The Defiant Muse

GERMAN FEMINIST POEMS
FROM THE MIDDLE AGES
TO THE PRESENT

THE DEFIANT MUSE
Series Editor, Angel Flores

The Defiant Muse: German Feminist Poems from the Middle Ages to the Present
Edited and with an introduction by Susan L. Cocalis

The Defiant Muse: Hispanic Feminist Poems from the Middle Ages to the Present
Edited and with an introduction by Angel Flores and Kate Flores

The Defiant Muse: French Feminist Poems from the Middle Ages to the Present
Edited and with an introduction by Domna C. Stanton

The Defiant Muse: Italian Feminist Poems from the Middle Ages to the Present
Edited by Beverly Allen, Muriel Kittel, and Keala Jane Jewell and with an introduction by Beverly Allen

The Defiant Muse

GERMAN FEMINIST POEMS
FROM THE MIDDLE AGES
TO THE PRESENT

A BILINGUAL ANTHOLOGY

EDITED AND WITH AN INTRODUCTION
BY SUSAN L. COCALIS

THE FEMINIST PRESS
AT THE CITY UNIVERSITY OF NEW YORK
NEW YORK

© 1986 by Susan L. Cocalis
All rights reserved. Published 1986
Printed in the United States of America

89 88 87 86   6 5 4 3 2 1

Permission acknowledgments begin on page 165.

Cover and text design by Gilda Hannah
Typeset by Weinglas Typography Inc.
Manufactured by Banta Company.

This publication is made possible, in part, by public
funds from the New York State Council on the Arts.

Library of Congress Cataloging-in-Publication Data
German feminist poems from the Middle Ages to
the present.
    (The Defiant muse)
    English and German.
    1. Feminism—poetry. 2. German poetry—
women authors—Translations into
English. 3. German poetry—Women
authors. 4. English poetry—Translations from
English. I. Cocalis, Susan L. II. Series.
PT1160.E5G38 1986   831'.008'09287   86-4774
ISBN 0-935312-49-8
ISBN 0-935312-53-6 (pbk.)

So then, to tell my story, here I stand.
The dress's tint, though bleached in bitter lye,
Has not all washed away. It still is real.
I call then with a thin, ethereal cry.

You hear me speak. But do you hear me feel?

Gertrud Kolmar

CONTENTS

PUBLISHER'S PREFACE

The Feminist Press is proud to publish this set of anthologies of feminist poetry, the first bilingual collection of its kind. When Domna C. Stanton proposed the project to The Press in 1983, I immediately responded that it was "a natural" for The Press, and a critical publication in women's studies that was long overdue. To be sure, the idea for the series and the actual work began years earlier. In 1976, Kate Flores urged Angel, her husband, to collaborate on an anthology, not simply of women's poetry, which had been sporadically included in the more than twenty volumes of verse he had edited, but specifically of feminist poetry, which had never been done. However, as the enormity of the undertaking became apparent, they enlarged the original scope from one to four volumes, each to be devoted to a major language, and contacted Domna C. Stanton for French, Susan L. Cocalis for German, and Beverly Allen and Muriel Kittel for Italian. In common, these editors agreed upon the general conception of the volumes; independently, over a period of several years, they did extensive research in libraries at home and in the countries of origin. That arduous process led to a "re-vision" of poets whose feminism had been ignored or suppressed. Far more important, it led to the discovery of numerous poets whose work remains unknown in their own country to this day. Thanks to these editors, the poetry can now have the audience it deserves.

Reading each volume produces the exciting awareness of a strong national tradition of feminist poetry, dating back to "the dark ages." Together, the anthologies confirm the existence of many common themes and threads that connect women beyond differences of class and culture, time and place. For that inspiring vision, the editors of this series, like those of us at The Feminist Press, can be proud...and joyful.

Florence Howe

INTRODUCTION

Perhaps one of the most important things to keep in mind when approaching a collection of feminist poetry is that the reader must suspend all previously learned and instinctively applied aesthetic criteria, as well as any preconceptions about the meaning of the term "feminist literature" in order to reach a deeper understanding of the emancipatory nature and poetic accomplishment of the texts presented.

In poetry written by German women throughout the centuries, the attribute "feminist" describes nuances, or thematic or formal aberrations from traditional norms, or lapses that suggest a new consciousness of the poet's situation as a woman, and specifically, as a woman writer. Thematically, this aberration can be found in a woman's defense of her writing; in the way that she approaches themes beyond the allegedly female domains of love, sentiment, religion, and the family; in her attempt to redefine herself, her relationship to men, her sexuality, or her role in society; in her anger or resentment at her "lot in life"; and in the way she feels alienated or displaced from the traditionally female sphere. Formally, it can be discovered in the poet's refusal to restrict herself to the poetic genres traditionally allotted to German women writers (hymns, psalms, love songs, spirituals, and, eventually, sonnets and odes); in an unexpected combination of form and theme (spiritual love songs); in an innovative use of imagery and metaphor through which the writer is searching for new ways to define herself without recourse to the literary images usually associated with women (angel in the house, muse, femme fatale, witch, eternal feminine); and in the conscious parody or ironic devaluation of such traditional images.

In order to understand the emancipatory nature of some of these texts, one must therefore begin to read them for what they do *not* say and how they are *not* written as much as for what they do say and how they appear. For feminist poetry, as one finds it in the texts of German women writers, often consists of a refusal to perpetuate oppressive structures of thought, themes, genres, images—or women's silence itself. The nature of this refusal changes in the course of centuries as women make some gains and formulate new demands, but it is always present in some form. The subtle interplay between articulation and silence, acceptance and refusal, tradition and innovation imbues many of these texts with a life and an aesthetic context of their own.

From the Middle Ages to the late eighteenth century, when more and more women were accepted by their male contemporaries as authors of lyric poetry, songs, and novels, the main struggle women faced as writers was that of being allowed to write at all. The earliest known women writers—Roswitha von Gandersheim in the tenth century and the great female mystics of the twelfth, thirteenth, and fourteenth centuries—Hildegard von Bingen, Elisabeth von Schönen, Gertrud von Helfta, Mechthild von Hackeborn, **Mechthild von Magdeburg*** (1210–1285), Elisabeth Stagel, and Margarethe Ebner—apologized for writing, but were essentially tolerated as women writing for other women. As such, they did not pose a threat to the Church or to the State. They were literate women living in cloisters as nuns or Beguines who were entrusted with the education and the religious instruction of the younger women of their order. As a result, Mechthild von Magdeburg records that she was warned that her manuscripts might be confiscated and burned as heretical, but she persevered, trusting in God, feeling she was writing at God's behest. And what God evidently bade Magdeburg to write were highly erotic love songs addressed to God himself, a male persona, or to the spirit of love, *Minne*, a female persona. This type of religious *Minnelied* was typical of other poetry written by German women mystics of this period. To the extent such poetry remained within the confines of convent life, being passed from generation to generation of women, the authors were not persecuted and many of the manuscripts survived.

During the Reformation and throughout the sixteenth century, however, such women as **Argula von Grumbach** (1492–1554), who entered the public arena with poetry supporting the Protestant cause, were viciously attacked by Catholic men for their efforts. In extreme cases, like that of Annelein von Freiburg, women were persecuted by the Inquisition and burned at the stake as heretics. By the seventeenth century, Protestant women from the upper social strata—the Countesses Aemilie Juliane, Ludämila Elisabeth von Schwarzberg-Rudolstadt, and Anna-Sophia von Hessen, Elisabeth von Braunschweig-Lüneburg, **Anna Owena Hoyers** (1584–1655), and Magdalena Haymeier, who all wrote religious poetry—were also tolerated by their peers. This may be attributed both to their social standing and to the new need for devotional songs in the Protestant liturgy. But regardless of social standing or need, these authors were tolerated only as long as they denied any self-awareness and presented themselves to the public as humble vessels of the Holy Spirit. The selection included here by Hoyers, with which she prefaced her collected poems in 1650, is a case in point.

In the late seventeenth and early eighteenth centuries, such apologetic introductions were still obligatory, but they reflected a new self-assertiveness of the authors. As was the case during the Reformation, women writers were attacked for neglecting their household responsibilities, for disturbing the moral order of the universe, and for getting in-

---

*The names of poets whose works are included in this volume appear in boldface type at first mention.

volved in matters that did not concern them. **Susanna Elisabeth Zeidler** (c. 1686), **Christiana Mariana von Ziegler** (1695–1760), and **H. E. Weichmann** (eighteenth century) responded to such charges by asserting their ability both to write and to perform their household duties, by defending women's creative powers, or by attacking male prejudices as such, if they bothered to defend themselves at all. Many simply allowed well-meaning male relatives, who were probably trying to avert a family scandal, to attest to their virtues, their domestic performance, and their humility. The new self-confidence of women writers of this time may also be seen in their mastery of the traditionally male poetic forms—the sonnet, the elegy, and the ode. As opposed to their predecessors, who saw themselves as mere vessels to be filled by the Holy Spirit, these women took pride in their own learning and extolled the virtues of such learned or extraordinary women as Anna Maria von Schurmann or Queen Anne. At this time, too, some of these women were recognized by male contemporaries for their achievements. **Catharina Regina von Greiffenberg** (1633–1694), Gertraud Moeller, and Ziegler were invited to join learned societies and clubs that had previously been closed to women; Ziegler and **Sidonie Hedwig Zäunemann** (1714–1740) were crowned poet laureates by universities; and **Anna Louisa Karsch** (1722–1791) was celebrated at the Prussian court. Some of them, like Zäunemann, also went to the extreme of appearing in society in men's clothing or blatantly living a life of sin, although most of them tried to maintain a feminine appearance so as not to endanger the gains they had made. Most of the poetry of these women falls into the category of religious literature or occasional poetry composed for births, deaths, birthdays, marriages, coronations, and military victories, but as the selections by Karsch, Zeidler, Ziegler, and Zäunemann demonstrate, these writers sometimes speak of themselves as individuals and of the plight of women in general. In such poems they tentatively voice their needs for more freedom from the constraints placed upon them by society: Greiffenberg rejects the bondage of love, Zäunemann extols celibacy, and Ziegler lambasts the social prejudices of the male sex. As Gisela Brinker-Gabler has pointed out, one can also witness the rudiments of a female solidarity among these women. They were aware of each other's existence and they began writing poetry to and for each other. Ziegler corresponded with Frau Bressler and **Anna Helena Volckmann** (c. 1736), Zäunemann with Frau Gutemund, and Frau Walther with Frau Löber in this manner. Later in the century, when Sophie von La Roche and Sophie Mereau initiated the first journals published by women for a specifically female audience, German women poets could be integrated into a newly evolving female literary community. The possibilities for publication multiplied after Friederike Helene Unger began managing her family's publishing house and after Therese Forster-Huber became the first woman editor of an established newspaper early in the nineteenth century.

During the course of the nineteenth century, the presence of women in the literary sphere and the existence of a definite female literary continuum became more and more pronounced. Younger generations of women writers referred explicitly to such female role models as La Roche, Mereau, and Unger, or expressed their admiration for the often notoriously emancipated lifestyles of women associated with the German Romantic movement, such as Dorothea Veit-Schlegel, Caroline Schlegel-Schelling, Therese Forster-Huber, Henriette Herz, Rahel Varnhagen, and Bettina von Arnim. At any rate, the process of rethinking woman's nature, her sexuality, and her role in society that had begun in the eighteenth century continued in much of the literature of this period. During the Romantic era, this attempt at redefinition is more or less implicit in the poems of Louise Brachmann, **Karoline von Günderode** (1780–1806), Bettina von Arnim, or, later in the century, in those of **Ida Hahn-Hahn** (1805–1880) and **Annette von Droste-Hülshoff** (1797–1848). As such, the poems included here by Günderode, Hahn-Hahn, and Droste-Hülshoff must be read more for what they do not contain than for their stated themes. Taking refuge in nature, a nocturnal realm, and a mythological world of her own creation, Günderode rejects the prosaic, diurnal realities of a woman's domestic and conjugal responsibilities in order to live out her passionate sexual fantasies. She rejects the domestic sphere, sees herself as a creative genius, and never stops to question whether society would find that role appropriate for a woman. Hahn-Hahn and Droste-Hülshoff, who also reject the domestic sphere, speak in less passionate terms and tend to sublimate their personal demands and wishes into descriptions of such gynomorphized natural phenomena as birds and rivers. Droste-Hülshoff also shows an inclination to disappear behind male personae in order to articulate traditionally non-feminine needs.

In the mid-nineteenth century, **Kathinka Zitz-Halein** (1801–1877), Louise von Plönnies, **Louise Aston** (1814–1871), **Louise Otto-Peters** (1819–1895), Emma Herwegh, Marie Kurz, and Mathilda Franziska Anneke were influenced by the various liberal and radical movements of the 1830s and 1840s and began writing more explicitly emancipatory poetry. For these writers, who published their works in political periodicals—often ones that they themselves edited until prohibited to do so by the German government—poetry was a valuable weapon in the struggle for the liberation of their sex and of all oppressed people. At mid-century the first women's organizations were formed and the first *Frauenzeitungen* (women's newspapers) began to appear. At first these focused on the issues of the legal rights of bourgeois women, arranged marriages, and the right to an education, but as the century progressed and more and more women from the working class became involved, the focus broadened to include the issues of oppressive working conditions, social welfare, and, eventually, anti-militarism and the right to vote. This is not to say, however, that the German women's movement as a whole espoused all of these causes, for there was no cohesive women's movement in Germany: there was a bourgeois movement and a socialist movement, each with its own issues and organizational apparatus. The poetry of the second half of the nineteenth and the early twentieth centuries reflects this diversity of interests and issues. Aston and Otto-Peters and the working-class writers **Emma Döltz** (1866–1950) and **Klara Müller-Jahnke** (1860–1905) write explicitly emancipatory, militant poems demanding an end to the oppression of women or describing the oppressive realities of working women in naturalistic detail. Zitz-Halein, **Betty Paoli** (1814–1894), **Marie von Ebner-Eschenbach** (1830–1916), **Marie Janitschek** (1859–1927), **Margarete Beutler** (1876–1949), and **Berta Lask** (1878–1967) depict the alienation felt by women as individuals; the dilemma of "modern women," bluestockings, or sexually liberated women; and the rebellion of the dolls, the painted madonnas, and the fallen women. **Ida von Reinsberg-Düringsfeld** (1815–1876) and **Marie von Najmájer** (1844–1904) extol the virtues of exemplary, sexually and politically liberated women like George Sand, Sappho, or Jeanne Manon Philipon-Roland. They all, however, express dissatisfaction with the social status quo, indicate an awareness of the particular forms of oppression that women experience, and suggest ways in which that situation could be changed.

These tendencies can be regarded as representative parts of an evolving tradition of women's poetry that had also come to be acknowledged as such by later generations of women. Much of the poetry written by women in the twentieth century may be characterized in the same way. Here too one finds evidence of neo-Romantic mythical realms, descriptions of gynomorphized natural phenomena, explicitly feminist texts, naturalistic vignettes, attempts at redefining women's role in society, and a new exploration of female sexuality. In the first half of the century, for example, **Gertrud Kolmar** (1894–1943?) and Else Lasker-Schüler, Jewish poets, pick up the Romantic tradition and create their own mythological realms in which they can play out their sexual and religious fantasies. In Kolmar's case, the scene of her fantasies is often a primitive barbaric or oriental world; in Lasker-Schüler's, it is a sensually lush biblical or oriental milieu. In both cases these realms predate Western culture and allow the poet an active, often androgynous existence otherwise denied her. This is not, however, a general tendency among Jewish women poets writing at that time, although one does encounter it in a slightly different form in the works of Nelly Sachs, Rose Ausländer, and **Mascha Kaléko** (1912–1975). Kaléko provides witty, ironic descriptions of petit-bourgeois life in Berlin during the Weimar Republic. There, love can only be expressed in shorthand on one's afternoon off. The lush oriental sensuality of Kolmar's and Lasker-Schüler's poetry cannot be accommodated in Kaléko's *Lyrical Stenographer's Notebook*.

In the poetry of the immediate post-war years, there is a prevailing sense of pessimism about the ability of the sexes—or of human beings at all—to communicate with each other. **Marie Luise Kaschnitz** (1901–1974), **Ingeborg Bachmann** (1926–1973), Friederike Mayröcker, Hilde Domin, Ilse Aichinger, and **Gabriele Wohmann** (1932–) take stock of their situation and record their alienation. Bachmann creates a dense, often mystical metaphorical context, reifying natural phenomena into stark images in order to voice despair. Kaschnitz often sustains a single metaphor through a scene to depict the relations between the sexes. Wohmann simply confronts the reader with a naturalistic picture of the bleak realities of women's lives. In such poems, a negative situation is allowed to speak for itself.

More explicitly feminist poetry did not become popular again until the 1970s, when, as a result of the contemporary women's movement, socially critical poetry began appearing in feminist periodicals and in editions sponsored by new feminist and leftist presses. Such writers as **Ute Erb** (1940–), **Helga Novak** (1935–), and **Ursula Krechel** (1947–) criticize the ''deficiencies'' in bourgeois society from a socialist perspective. **J. Monika Walther** (1945–), **Karin Kiwus** (1942–), and **Angelika Mechtel** (1943–) question the perpetuation of certain domestic routines, bourgeois attitudes, or social institutions that enslave and eventually deform women and children. Kiwus and **Barbara Fiedler** (1942–) demand a revision of history to include *her*story, while **Maria Neef-Uthoff** (1947–) and **Sigrid Ammer** (n.d.) speculate about their relationship to their mothers and to their maternal heritage. **Sigrid Weigel** (1950–), **Helga Osswald** (1942–), and **Frederike Frei** (1945–) pose problems reflecting the contradictions inherent in the present women's movement, and readers must come up with their own answers. **Verena Stefan** (1947–) and **Margot Schroeder** (1937–) rebel openly against male sexual domination and celebrate lesbian sexuality. Contemporary feminists invoke Anna Akhmátova, Medea, and Angela Davis. They have organized and now run their own journals and presses as a result of a more cohesive women's movement that developed around the issue of a woman's right to control her own body. And contemporary feminists have begun exploring the full potential of hetero- and homosexuality as a means of a woman's self-fulfillment.

Women throughout the ages have been oppressed. That can be seen in the poetry collected here. They have also been aware of their oppression, or at least of their own dissatisfaction with their lot in life. Some women chose to combat that oppression openly, using their writing as a weapon in the struggle for women's liberation. Others rebelled by refusing to remain within the traditional confines of ''women's poetry'' or by the very act of writing poetry at all. But the awareness of their own alienation and the assertion of their own identity in writing make their poetry feminist poetry. Feminist poetry therefore does provide us with herstory, with texts documenting the historical forms of women's oppression and gradual emancipation. But it also provides us with poetry, with the metaphors that bridge the gaps in history to provide us with a female literary continuum with its own traditions and aesthetic norms.

Gisela Brinker-Gabler's excellent anthology, *Deutsche Dichterinnen vom 16. Jahrhundert bis zur Gegenwart* (1978) was the source for many of the texts that appeared between 1650 and 1950, for biographical information, and for bibliographical references to earlier women poets. Her introduction was also helpful in suggesting the location of some of the poets within the context of a female literary continuum. Cäcelia Friedrich's collection of socialist poetry by women, *Aus dem Schaffen früher sozialistischer Schrift-stellerinnen* (1966) has also been a much appreciated resource. Although the Staatsbibliothek Preußischer Kulturbesitz in West Berlin offered invaluable assistance in locating some of the earlier texts, many of the more promising titles could not be found. The opposite problem presented itself with the contemporary texts: There were so many volumes of new feminist poetry on the shelves of the women's bookstores in West Berlin that the process of selection was difficult.

In all cases, the poems appear in their original orthography. In translating these texts for this volume, the editor and her collaborator for the earlier poems, Gerlinde Geiger, attempted to maintain the meter, rhyme scheme, and idiom of the German poem, taking some liberties in rendering German images or colloquial phrases into their English equivalents. Therefore, although the meaning is reproduced in the English version, the poems are not literal, word-for-word translations of the original.

The Defiant Muse

GERMAN FEMINIST POEMS
FROM THE MIDDLE AGES
TO THE PRESENT

VON DIESEM BUCHE

Ich ward vor diesem Buch gewarnt,
und ward mir von Menschen also gesagt:
Wollte man es nicht bewahren,
es könnte ein Brand drüberfahren.—
Da tat ich, wie ich von Kind an getan,
wenn ich betrübt war. Ich fing zu beten an
und neigte mich und sprach zu meinem Lieb:
Eia, Herr, nun bin ich betrübt.
Durch Deine Ehre soll ich nun ungetröstet von Dir bleiben,
Du hast mich verleitet,
Du hießest mich selbst, es zu schreiben!—
Da hat sich Gott zu meiner Seele gewandt
und hielt dies Buch in seiner rechten Hand
und sprach: Meine Liebste, betrübe Dich nicht zu sehr,
die Wahrheit verbrennt niemand und nimmermehr.
Wer mir dies Buch aus der Hand will nehmen,
der muß stärker sein denn ich.
Dreifaltig ist dies Buch
und bezeichnet alleine Mich!

VON GÖTTLICHER MINNE KRAFT

Eia, liebe Gottesminne, umhalse stets die Seele mein,
Tod wär es mir mit tiefstem Weh,
müßt ich von Dir freie sein.
Eia, Minne, laß mich nicht erkühlen,
meine Werke sind all tot,
darf ich Dich nicht fühlen.
O Minne! Süße machst Du Pein und Not,
gibst Lehr und Trost den wahren Gotteskindern.
O Minneband!
Deiner süßen Hand ist die Gewalt,
sie bindet beide, jung und alt.
O Minne! Du machst große Bürden leicht,
und kleine Sünde schwer Dich deucht.

MECHTHILD VON MAGDEBURG (1210–1285)

ABOUT THIS BOOK

I was warned about this book,
and people spoke to me as follows:
they did not want to keep it there
for over it a blaze might flare.
Then I acted, as from childhood I've done,
when I'm grieved. I began an orison
and knelt down saying to my dear:
Oh, please, Lord, now I'm troubled here.
In Your honor I'm bereft of solace,
You've led me astray,
You Yourself have made me acquiesce.
Then God turned and gave my soul a look
and in His hand He held this book
and said: My dearest, do not grieve too much,
no one will ever burn the truth as such.
Whoever takes this book from me
must be stronger than I've been.
This book is in three parts
and describes myself alone therein!

—*S.L. Cocalis*

ON THE DIVINE POWER OF COURTLY LOVE

Oh, sweet courtly love of God, always clasp the soul in me,
It would be death in mortal pain
if free of you I had to be.
Oh, love, do not let me ever grow cold,
all of my works would then be dead
were I no longer to feel your hold.
Oh, sweet love! You cause distress and dread,
but teach God's children, offer solace.
Oh, love's bonds!
Your sweet hand can strike
both the young and old alike.
Oh, love! You make all our burdens light
but little sins do not seem slight.

Du dienest gerne ohne Entgelt,
hast Dich unter alle Kreaturen gestellt.—
Eia, süße Gottesminne, wenn ich allzulange schlafe
in Versäumnis guter Dinge,
so tu wohl und wecke mich und singe
mir, Fraue, Deinen Sang,
da Du die Seel' mitrührest
gleich süßem Saitenklang.
Eia, liebe Frau, wirf mich unter Dich,
viel gerne werde ich sieglos.
Darin, dass Du mir das Leben nimmst,
Fraue, liegt ja all mein Trost.

AIN ANTWORT IN GEDICHTH, AINEM AUF DER HOHEN SCHUL ZU INGOLSTAT AUFF AINEN SPRUCH, NEWLICH VON IM AUFGANGEN, WELCHER SYNDEN DABEI GETRUKT STEET

SCHRIFT GEGEN ARGULA

Fraw Argel arg ist ewer nam
Vil ärger, daß ir one scham
Und alle weyblich Zucht vergessen
So freuel seyt und so vermessen
Daß ir ewer Fürsten und Herren
Erst wöllt aynen newer glawben lernen
Und euch daneben understeet
Ayn gantze Universitet
Zustraffen und zuschumpffieren
Mit ewerm närrischen Allegieren. [. . .]
So stell ab dein Mut und gutdunckel
Und spinn darfür an deiner gunckel
Oder strick hauben und Werk bortten
Ein weyb soll nit mit Gottes wortten
Stoltzieren, und die Menner leren
Sonder mit Magdalenen zuhören
Ich gib euch fraw ein gutten rath
Und ob ir mein nit kundtschafft hatt

You serve without remuneration
all creatures of God's own creation'—
oh, sweet love of God, if I should sleep,
forget to do good things,
please wake me up and sing
to me, oh, woman dear, your song.
Since you would touch my soul
like the sweet chords of strings.
Oh, dear woman, cast me to the ground,
I shall be happy to lose to you.
The fact that you have won the final round,
oh, woman, will be a source of solace too.

—S.L. Cocalis

ARGULA VON GRUMBACH (1492–1554)

AN ANSWER IN VERSE FOR SOMEONE STUDYING IN INGOLSTADT IN ANSWER TO SOME VERSES THAT HE WROTE RECENTLY: WHICH TRANSGRESSIONS HE LISTS THERE

VERSES AGAINST ARGULA
Mme. Argel, awful is your name
Much worse that you—without shame—
And forgetting ev'ry female trait
Are so wicked, such an apostate
That you would teach your sovereign
The new dogma through your pen.
And then you have the impudence
To punish and abuse students
And the university
With your dumb prolixity. [. . .]
So curb your mettle and your zeal
And go back to your spinning wheel
Or go knit caps and do lacework
A woman shouldn't flaunt God's word
And try to teach the men.
She should keep still like Mary Magdalen.
I'm giving you good counsel
And if you want to know I'll tell

So bin ich Joannes genent
Zu Ingolstat ein frey student
Ain Bürgers sun von Lantzhut
Habt mit aym schuler so vergut
Und khommet mit dyser sach nit wider
Ir lygt mit allen ewern ketzern nider.

ANTWORT DER ARGULA
In gottes namen heb ich an
zu antworten dem künen man
Der sich Joannem nennen thut
Zaygt mir an er sey von Lantzhut
Daß ich wißz zuerkennen in. [. . .]
Seyt ir ain redlich Christlich man
Zu Ingolstat trett auff den plan
Auff eynen tag der euch gefelt
Hab ich geirrt, das selb erzelt.
So ir mir gottes wort her bringt
Volg ich, wie ain gehorsam kyndt
Zaygt mir mein irrsall redlich an
Wie sich gepürt aym Christen man
Dar vor drey wochen oder vier
Den selben tag ernennet mir
Damit auch ander khommen her
Zuhören was mein sach da wer
Gar fröhlich will ich zu euch gan
Seyt das triff gott mein Herren an
Christus gibt mir gar feyn bericht
Wie ich mir auch soll fürchten nicht
So ich gleich fürgestellet wer
Sein Vatter geb uns selbs die leer
Schickt uns sein gayst in unsern mundt
Der redt für uns zu dyser stundt
Ir seyt nit die ir reden seyt
Ja dyses wort mein hertz erfrewt
Ob ich gleich kayn geschriffte kan
Kayn schrecken hab ich gar daran
Will zu euch khommen on beschwer
Dem namen gots zu lob und eer. [. . .]

My name's Johannes and I'm free,
I study at the university
Of Ingolstadt and I come from Landshut.
So take a student's word in this dispute
And don't bring this up again.
You and your kind will be defeated then.

ARGULA'S ANSWER
In God's name let me begin
To answer that audacious man
Who calls himself Johannes—
And so I'll know just who he is
He says that he's from Landshut. [...]
If you're honest and a Christian,
Show up in Ingolstadt, my friend,
On any day that you may care.
If I have erred, then say it there
And if you can make me see the light
I'll follow you without a fight.
Show me where I've gone astray
And do so in a Christian way.
Just name the day and circumstance
Three weeks, four weeks in advance
So that more people can attend
To hear how I myself defend.
I will undertake the task with glee
Since it's for God and not for me.
Christ Himself has let me know
That I should not be afraid to go
Since I will represent Him well.
His Father gives us words Himself,
He sends His spirit to our words,
He speaks for us; He is heard.
You do not see whom you seem to see.
Yes, this message gladdens me.
Although I am not educated
I am not afraid to say it.
I will come and without fear
To honor God, whom I revere. [...]

—S.L. Cocalis

AN DEN CHRISTLICHEN LESER

Dieses Buch dürch eine Fraw beschribn,
Wird man gwiß darumb mehr beliebn,
Weiln dergleichen nie gesehn,
Von Frawn so geistreich ausgehn.
Man wolls nur lesen und betrachtn
Und auff der Spötter Red nicht achtn,
Die da sagen: es sey nicht fein.
Christus ja meist Mariam preist,
Ob schon Martha ihm kocht und speist,
Weiln sie erwehlt das beste Theil,
In dehm sie gesucht der Seelen Heil.
Wie diese Fraw auch hat gethan,
Als darvon diß Buch zeugen kan,
Das auch die Weisheit nicht zuholln
Von Welt-Gelehrten und Hohen-Schuln,
Sondern vom Heyligen Geist allein
Mus erbeten und gelernet sein.
Gott woll das sich niemand wol schämm
Von Frawn guth Exempel zu nehmn.
Wollst nur leser diß perlegirn
Und darnach darvon Iudicirn.
Der Heyliger Geist dich illustrirn
Und dich zum Reich Gottes recht führ.
Amen.

GEGEN AMOR

Der kleine Wüterich mag mit den Pfeilen spielen
und tändeln, wie er will: er gewinnet mir nichts ab,
weil gegen seine Pfeil ein Demant Herz ich hab.
Er machet mich nicht wund, ich darf nit Schmerzen fühlen.

ANNA OWENA HOYERS (1584–1655)

FOR THE CHRISTIAN READER

This book, by a woman writ,
Is the better because of it,
Because its like has ne'er been seen:
Wit and sense from woman's pen.
Just consider what you read
And to the scoffers pay no heed,
Who say it isn't right.
For Mary Christ his special praise reserved,
Even though Martha cooked and served,
Because she chose the better role
In that she chose to save the soul.
So does the present woman too
As this book will prove to you
That wisdom is not to be found
In colleges and learnèd rounds,
But from the Holy Ghost alone
Can the highest things be known.
God would have you feel no shame
If He speaks in woman's name.
And should you, readers, peruse this work
And thereupon decide its worth,
The Holy Spirit will illuminate
And lead you to the Pearly Gate.
Amen.

—*S.L. Cocalis*

CATHARINA REGINA VON GREIFFENBERG (1633–1694)

ANTI-CUPID

That ruthless little tyrant can trifle, flirt, and fling
his arrows as he pleases: I'll ward off his caress
for in this case, you see, a heart of stone I do possess.
He cannot wound me; I will not feel the sting.

Er mag mit tausend List auf meine Freyheit zielen
Ihm ich, dem blinden Kind, ein Zucker-Zeltlein gab:
er meint', es wär mein Herz. O leicht-geteuschter Knab!
Ich will mein Mütlein noch an deiner Einfalt kühlen.

Schau, wie gefällt dir das! trotz, spräng mir diesen Stein
mit deinem goldnen Pfeil. Der Lorbeer soll mich zieren,
nicht deine Dornen-Ros' und Myrten-Sträuchelein.

Du meinst es sey nur Scherz, ich wolle mich vexiren.
Nein! nein! die süße Ruh soll mir das Liebste seyn,
mein dapfers Herz soll nichts als Ruh und Freyheit spüren.

AIN EINEN GUTEN FREUND, WELCHER MIT
DER KÖNIGIN ANNA EXEMPEL DER WEIBER
UNBESTÄNDIGKEIT BEWEISEN WOLTE

Der Weiber Unbestand ist noch nicht gnug bewiesen,
Wenn Englands Anna nur zum Beyspiel dienen soll.
Drum wird, geehrter Freund, dich dieses nicht verdriessen,
Wenn dieser kleine Brieff ihr Thun entschuldgen soll.

Schau die Regierung an, die sie bißher geführet:
Thuts nicht ihr kluger Sinn gar vielen Männern vor?
Sie zeigte ihre Treu, wo sichs mit recht gebühret,
Wenn Ludwig als ein Mann so Schaam als Treu verlohr.

Sie hieß in aller Welt das Wunder dieser Zeiten.
Man wuste keine Frau, die iemahls so regiert.
Sie kunte um das Lob mit vielen Helden streiten,
Weil sie sich ie so klug als tapffer aufgeführt.

Der Friede krönte sie; sie war die Lust des Landes.
Ihr dreyfach grosses Reich war unter ihr recht frey.
Die Völcker freuten sich des angenehmen Bandes,
Weil ihre Königin drey Cronen würdig sey.

Die Nachbarn liebten sie, weil ihre Feinde bebten.
Europa hielte sie vor ein vollkomnes Gut,

With a thousand tricks and ruses he wants my independence.
To him, that blind child, I have given a confection:
He thought it was my heart, did not suspect deception!
But I will vent my anger on his inexperience.

Look, how do you like that! defy me, split this stone for me
with your golden arrow. I'll be adorned with laurel leaves,
not with your myrtle boughs and roses that are thorny.

You think it's just a joke, that I wish to tease.
No! No! Sweet repose is the most precious thing to me;
my brave heart is made for freedom and for peace.

—*S.L. Cocalis and G.M. Geiger*

MARGARETHA SUSANNA VON KUNTSCH (1651–1716)

TO A GOOD FRIEND WHO WOULD PROVE THE FICKLENESS OF WOMEN WITH THE EXAMPLE OF QUEEN ANNE*

The fickleness of women can not be fully proved
If one only cites the case of England's Anne.
Therefore, honored friend, do not be falsely moved
If this little letter makes excuses for her stand.

Look at the government in which she has prevailed.
Does she not surpass men through her intelligence?
Whenever it was called for, her fealty she unveiled,
While Louis—as a man—had lost his moral sense.

Renowned in all the world as a female protégé,
There had never been a queen who'd ruled with such control.
She could vie for fame with the heroes of her day
Because she'd always been as smart as she was bold.

Concord crowned her head, she was the welfare of her nation.
In her three-fold realm she let freedom's rule abound.
The people all enjoyed such pleasant subjugation
Because they knew their queen was graced to wear three crowns.

The neighbors loved her too because her foes decreased.
All Europe thought she was the model of a queen,

Weil durch sie Könige und Fürsten ruhig lebten.
Ja ieder Theil der Welt wust ihren Löwen-Muth.

Kurtz, was der gröste Held und König kan erlangen,
Das traf man wundersam bey unsrer Anna an.
Es kont ihr hohes Haupt mit solchen Gütern prangen,
Die kaum der zehnde Mann mit Müh erlangen kan.

Das machte ihre Treu und ihr beständigs Wesen
Und daß sie selbst regiert, dahero irrstu dich,
Mein Freund, indem dein Brief das Widerspiel läst lesen.
Es ist ein falscher Rath, nicht sie, veränderlich.

Fürwahr du schlägst dich selbst mit deinen eignen Worten,
Weil du von Annen schreibst, was Männer doch gethan.
Was Bullingbrock verübt, und dessen Schand-Consorten,
Geht nicht die Königin und ihr Gemüthe an.

Sie hat es zwar versehn, daß sie zu viel getrauet,
Doch mein Freund, wer ist wohl frey vor übertünchter List.
Da viele Könige auf Diener Treu gebauet,
Die endlich zum Betrug und Falschheit worden ist.

Ich wolte also wohl mit besserm Rechte sagen,
Das weibliche Geschlecht sey standhafft, fromm und treu.
Man könte über euch mit mehrerm Gründe klagen,
Daß kaum von hunderten ein Mann beständig sey.

Allein ich will das nicht; ich schone dein Geschlechte,
Da du, geehrter Freund, voll Treu und Ehrlichkeit,
Und mache diesen Schluß: Die Treue heist mit Rechte
Bey Manns- und Weibes-Volck die gröste Seltenheit.

Hiemit beschliesse ich die wenigen Gedancken.
Gefallen sie dir nun, so ändre deinen Sinn;
Doch wirst du auch gleich nicht von deiner Meynung wancken,
So wisse, daß ich dir mit Treu ergeben bin.*

*The original poem was not divided into strophes.

Since under her aegis kings and princes lived in peace.
To all the world she was the lion-hearted queen.

Indeed, that which the greatest king and hero could attain,
That all was manifest in England's heroine.
On her lofty brow such excellence was plain
That not one man in ten could ever hope to win.

Her constancy it was and her steadfast nature
And that she reigned herself, so therefore you have erred,
My friend, in your letter's use of nomenclature:
Not she, it is false counsel, to whom your charge referred.

Indeed, you paint yourself with your false reports,
Because you censure Anne for things that men have done:
Crimes Bolingbroke** committed along with shameful consorts
Do not concern Queen Anne nor her disposition.

Granted, she has erred by too much trust and confidence.
Yet, my friend, who's safe from shewdly veiled deceit?
Since many kings rely on servants' blind obedience,
Which may be used against them if servants lie and cheat.

I'd therefore like to say, and it may be more correct,
That the female sex is constant, good, and true.
One could complain of men, and rightly I'd suspect,
That not one in a hundred could be called constant too.

But I shall spare your sex; I don't want to complain,
Since you, my honored friend, are constant and sincere.
Thus I must conclude: constancy, as people claim,
Is something all too rare among both sexes here.

And thus I will conclude my comments on this matter.
If they should please you, friend, I beg you change your view.
But even if you feel you cannot do the latter,
Then know that I'll remain bound faithfully to you.

—*S.L. Cocalis and G.M. Geiger*

*Queen Anne Stuart (1665–1714)
**Henry St. John Bolingbroke was a British statesman, orator, and writer (1678–1751).

BEGLAUBIGUNG DER JUNGFER POETEREY

Rhapsodius glaubt nicht das Jungfern Verse machen:
Wie solte man nu nicht der falschen Meynung lachen?
Wie, wenn man sagte, das hochzeitliche Gedicht,
Das Rhapsodus gemacht, ist seine Arbeit nicht.

Ist dieses müglich, so kan jenes auch geschehen.
Hat denn Herr Rhapsodus dergleichen nie gesehen?
Ihr Musen Söhne denckt, ihr seyd es gar allein,
Bey denen Phoebus zeucht mit seinen Künsten ein.

O nein, ihr irret euch: Die Pallas pflegt desgleichen
Kunst, Weißheit und Verstand uns Nimphen darzureichen.
Sind wir gleich nicht an Kunst und Gaben gar zu reich,
Noch euch, ihr Phoebus Volck in allen Stücken gleich.

(Denn dieses ist gewiß, das läßt man wol passiren,
Das euch die freye Kunst vortrefflich kan beziren.
Dazu euch euer Fürst Apollo Anlaß giebt,
Wenn ihr von Jugend auf Parnassus Hügel liebt.)

So werdet ihr doch diß nicht gäntzlich leugnen können,
Das Gott und die Natur uns ebenmäßig gönnen.
Was euch gegen ist, und das uns offtmahls nicht
Das Tichten, sondern nur die Zeit dazu gebricht.

Es fehlt uns nicht an Witz und andern guten Gaben,
Nur das man nicht dazu Gelegenheit kan haben.
Wenn man uns so wie euch, die Künste gösse ein,
So wolten wir euch auch hierinnen gleicher seyn.

SUSANNA ELISABETH ZEIDLER (c. 1686)

VERIFICATION OF THE POETIC TALENTS OF YOUNG MAIDENS

The Rhapsodist cannot believe that maidens can make verse!
One cannot avoid rejecting his opinion as perverse!
It is as if one said that the wedding hymn
Made by the rhapsodist was not a poem by him.

If one is possible, the other can exist.
Have you never seen the like, Mr. Rhapsodist?
You sons of muses think that Phoebus did impart
To you and to you only the precious gift of art.

Oh no, you are mistaken: Athena tends to recompense
Us nymphs with the same—art, wisdom, and intelligence.
But all this notwithstanding, our talents are so modest
That we can never rival you, even with our goddess.

(For it is surely true, with talent you've been rendered.
Creative art adorns you in all its graceful splendor.
For in you your Prince Apollo will gracefully induce
Your love of Mt. Parnassus, in your early youth.)

This fact you'll surely not propose to disavow:
That God and Nature also women do endow
With the same poetic talents which in us you attack.
It's not poetic talents, it's the time for them we lack.

Wit we do not lack, nor any other trait,
But we don't have the chance these to articulate.
Were we the same as you in the arts immersed
Then we would surely be quite equally well-versed.

—*S.L. Cocalis and G.M. Geiger*

DAS MÄNNLICHE GESCHLECHTE, IM NAMEN
EINIGER FRAUENZIMMER BESUNGEN

Du Weltgepriesenes Geschlechte,
Du in dich selbst verliebte Schaar,
Prahlst allzusehr mit deinem Rechte,
Das Adams erster Vorzug war.
Doch soll ich deinen Werth besingen,
Der dir auch wirklich zugehört;
So wird mein Lied ganz anders klingen,
Als das, womit man dich verehrt.

Ihr rühmt das günstige Geschicke,
Das euch zu ganzen Menschen macht;
Und wißt in einem Augenblicke
Worauf wir nimmermehr gedacht.
Allein; wenn wir euch recht betrachten,
So seyd ihr schwächer als ein Weib.
Ihr müßt oft unsre Klugheit pachten,
Noch weiter als zum Zeitvertreib.

Kommt her, und tretet vor den Spiegel:
Und sprechet selbst, wie seht ihr aus?
Der Bär, der Löwe, Luchs, und Igel
Sieht bey euch überall heraus.
Vergebt, ich muß die Namen nennen,
Wodurch man eure Sitten zeigt.
Ihr mögt euch selber wohl nicht kennen,
Weil man von euren Fehlern schweigt.

Seht doch wie ihr vor Eifer schäumet,
Wenns nicht nach eurem Kopfe geht.
O Himmel, was ist da versäumet,
Wenn man nicht gleich zu Diensten steht?
Ihr flucht mit fürchterlicher Stimme,
Als kämt ihr aus des Pluto Kluft.
Und wer entgehet Eurem Grimme,
Wenn ihr das Haus zusammen ruft?

Die, welche sich nur selbst erheben,
Die gerne groß und vornehm sind,
Nach allen Ehrenämtern streben,
Da doch den Kopf nichts füllt als Wind:
Die keine Wissenschaften kennen,
Und dringen sich in Würden ein,

CHRISTIANA MARIANA VON ZIEGLER (1695–1760)

IN PRAISE OF THE MALE SEX, AS SEEN BY CERTAIN FEMALES

You males, praised the whole world through,
You charming, narcissistic crowd,
You flaunt your rights with much ado,
Rights with which Adam was endowed.
But should I laud your accomplishments
With words you are entitled to,
Then you'd certainly note a difference
From other songs that praise you.

You say that fortune's favored you
By making you someone complete;
And in a wink you can construe
Thoughts with which we can't compete.
Yet if we'd investigate your privilege
You'd be found weaker by a measure;
You often borrow from our knowledge
More than is needed for your pleasure.

Come here, go to the mirror, stare:
And say yourself, what do you see?
The lion, lynx, the hedgehog, bear?
All those appear in there to me.
Excuse me, if such names I use—
To describe your manners as I must—
You probably have different views
Since your faults are ne'er discussed.

But look at how you rant and rave,
If things fail to go your way.
O Heavens, how you misbehave,
If one incurs a slight delay.
You utter dreadful imprecations
As if you'd just escaped from Hell,
And who has escaped your indignation
At the domestic personnel?

Those who claim to be superior,
Who think they're important and refined,
Who strive for titulary honor,
Though idle matters fill their mind:
They don't know any science
But still get titles and degrees;

Die kann man wohl mit Namen nennen,
Daß sie der Thorheit Kinder seyn.

Die Männer müssen doch gestehen,
Daß sie wie wir, auch Menschen sind.
Daß sie auch auf zwey Beinen gehen;
Und daß sich manche Schwachheit findt.
Sie trinken, schlafen, essen, wachen.
Nur dieses ist der Unterscheid,
Sie bleiben Herr in allen Sachen,
Und was wir thun, heißt Schuldigkeit.

Der Mann muß seine Frau ernähren,
Die Kinder, und das Hausgesind.
Er dient der Welt mit weisen Lehren,
So, wie sie vorgeschrieben sind.
Das Weib darf seinen Witz nicht zeigen:
Die Vorsicht hat es ausgedacht,
Es soll in der Gemeine schweigen,
Sonst würdet ihr oft ausgelacht.

Ihr klugen Männer schweigt nur stille:
Endecket unsre Fehler nicht.
Denn es ist selbst nicht unser Wille,
Daß euch die Schwachheit wiederspricht.
Trag eines nur des andern Mängel,
So habt ihr schon genug gethan,
Denn Menschen sind fürwahr nicht Engel,
An denen man nichts tadeln kann.

One must admit with all due deference:
They are fools with pedigrees.

Yet one day men too must confess,
That they are flesh and blood as we.
That they, as we, two legs possess
And are not free of infirmity.
They also eat, drink, sleep, and wake,
There only is one difference:
They are masters of their fate
While we serve in obedience.

The man must indeed support his wife,
The children, and domestic servants.
He teaches what he's learned in life
As is proscribed by ordinance.
The woman dare not show her intellect:
Providence decrees this too,
Our public silence you expect
Else we'd be making fun of you.

You clever men, now just be still
And overlook what we can't do.
For indeed it's not our will,
That the weak sex speaks up to you.
If we each other's faults would bear,
Then you would have done enough:
For people are not angels fair
And are made from weaker stuff.

—*S. L. Cocalis and G.M. Geiger*

JUNGFERN-GLÜCK

Niemand schwatze mir vom Lieben und von Hochzeitsmachen vor,
Cypripors Gesang und Liedern weyh ich weder Mund noch Ohr.
Ich erwehl zu meiner Lust eine Cutt- und Nonnen-Mütze,
Da ich mich in Einsamkeit wieder manches lästern schütze.
Ich will lieber Sauer-Kraut und die ungeschmeltzten Rüben.
In dem Kloster vor das Fleisch in dem Ehstands-Hause lieben.
Mein Vergnügen sey das Chor, wo ich sing und beten tuhe,
Denn dasselbe wirkt und schafft mir die wahre Seelen-Ruhe.
Will mir den gefaßten Schluß weder Mann noch Jüngling glauben,
Immerhin, es wird die Zeit euch doch diesen Zweifel rauben.
Geht nur hin, und sucht mit Fleiß Amors Pfeile, Amors Waffen,
Und geberdet euch darbey als wie die verliebten Affen!
Dorten stund in einem Carmen auf den Herrn von Obernütz:
Kriegt das schöne Jungfern-Röckgen einen Flecken, Ritz und Schlitz,
So muß auch der Jungfern Glück und die edle Freyheit weichen,
Und dargegen sucht die Angst sich gar eilend einzuschleichen.
Dieser Vers hat recht gesagt, Jungfern können kühnlich lachen;
Dahingegen manches Weib sich muß Angst und Sorge machen.
Kriegt die Noth durch Gegen-Mittel eine Lindrung und ein Loch,
Ey, so währt es doch nicht lange, und man schauet immer noch
Eben so viel Bitterkeit als in Erfurt Mannes Krausen,
Leid und Trübsal, Gram und Pein will die armen Weiber zausen.
Kriegt ein Weib von ihrem Mann manchen Tag ein Dutzend Mäulgen,
Ey! so sagt, was folgt darauf? Über gar ein kleines Weilgen
Brennt des Mannes Zorn wie Feuer, und er schwöret beym Parnaß:
Frau! ich werde dich noch prügeln, oder stecke dich ins Faß.
Dieser Weiber Noth und Pein will ich mich bey Zeit entschlagen,
Denn so darf kein Herzens-Wurm jemahls meine Seele nagen.
Drum so sag ich noch einmahl; Gute Nacht, du Scherz und Küssen,
Ich will deine Eitelkeit bis in meine Gruft vermissen.

SIDONIE HEDWIG ZÄUNEMANN (1714–1740)

A MAID'S FORTUNE

Let no one speak to me of love and matrimony, please,
Neither my lips nor ears shall grace Cyprian melodies.
For my earthly pleasure a cowl and nun's veil I choose
Because in my chaste solitude I'll be spared from much abuse.
Sauerkraut and raw turnips, convent fare, I would rather eat
Than in a conjugal house be served the choicest meat.
The choir is my amusement, in which I pray and sing,
For that is soothing and gives me a sense of true well-being.
Should neither man nor youth believe in my conviction,
It doesn't matter! Time will convince you of my prediction.
Go ahead and search for Cupid's weapons, Cupid's darts,
And in the process, act like apes who've lost their hearts!
In a song of Herr von Obernütz these verses one can hear:
If a fair maid's skirt should show soil, slit, or smear,
Then her freedom and good fortune will abandon her apace
And before you know it, fear will try to take their place.
This verse tells it as it is: A maid can laugh in all propriety,
While many a good wife must live with troubles and anxiety.
And assuming her distress should be lessened by some remedy,
Oh, this can't last too long before again you'll see
Just as much bitterness as there are frills for Erfurt's men:
Grief and misery, pain and suffering are a wife's daily regimen.
If on some days a wife receives a dozen kisses from her spouse,
Oh! tell me what will come of that? Before the day is out
His anger'll flare up like fire and by heathen gods he'll swear:
Wife, I'll thrash you soundly or I'll lock you up somewhere!
Such conjugal grief and suffering I've chosen to forego
Because I won't allow my heart to suffer so much woe.
Therefore I shall say again: Adieu to kisses and to jest!
I don't need your vanity while life beats in my breast.

—S.L. Cocalis and G.M. Geiger

ÜBER MADEMOISELLE WEICHMANN UNGEMEINE
GESCHICKLICHKEIT IN DER DICHT-KUNST WOLLTE
SEINE GEDANCKEN ERÖFNEN, UND SEINE HOCHACHTUNG
GEGEN DIESELBE BEZEUGEN, DERO WENIG BEKANNTER,
DOCH ERGEBNER DIENER, J.M. DARNMANN

Was Wunder seh' ich nun! Ich mögte fast erröhten;
Crönt doch die *Weichmannin* die Anzahl der Poeten.
Der Jungfern Zierd' ist sonst die Haushaltung verstehn;
Solls etwas mehrers seyn, Spiel, Tantzen, Sticken, Nehn.
Der Geist der *Weichmannin* will etwas edlers haben,
Den angebohrnen Trieb zu stillen und zu laben,
Als solche Kleinigkeit, die Nadel, Cart' und Tantz.
Wenn sie ja spielen will, flicht sie den Ehren-Crantz,
Der ihrer Stirn gebührt, mit Laub der Pierinnen,
Und steigt zum Zeit-Vertreib auf des Parnassus Zinnen.
Seh ich den muntern Schritt, so denck' ich dies dabey:
Daß sie gewiß nicht *Weich*, wol eine *Männin* sey.

HERRN DARNMANNS UNVERDIENTE HÖFLICHKEIT
WOLLTE, MIT BEYBEHALTUNG DER REIME, IN
FOLGENDEM BEANTWORTEN, DESSEN GEHORSAME
DIENERIN, H. E. WEICHMANN

Was Wunder seh' ich doch! wie! sollt' ich nicht erröhten?
Zählt mich Herr *Darnmann* denn nun gar zu den Poeten?
So ists! Sein muntrer Vers giebt höflich zu verstehn,
Ich könnte schon mit Recht in dieser Reihe gehn.
Allein ich kenne mich und meine schlechte Gaben.
Kann gleich die Poesie, nebst der Music mich laben;
So wag' ich mich dennoch nicht an den Dichter-Tantz,
Und lasse williglich den stoltzen Lorbeer-Crantz
Den Jungfern alter Zeit, den schlauen Pierinnen.
Mir siehts gefährlich aus auf des Parnassus Zinnen.
Seh' ich sein Gütig-seyn, so denck' ich dies dabey,
Daß den Poeten längst ein Schertz erlaubet sey.

H.E. WEICHMANN (EIGHTEENTH CENTURY)

WANTING TO AIR HIS THOUGHTS ABOUT AND PROVE HIS
RESPECT FOR MADEMOISELLE WEICHMANN'S UNUSUAL
TALENT IN THE ART OF POETRY, I REMAIN HER FAITHFUL
BUT LITTLE-KNOWN SERVANT, J. M. DARNMANN

What miracle is this! I almost blush, I know it;
Miss *Weichmann* adds the crowning touch to our class of poets.
A maiden always has been graced by domestic arts;
And if more is needed, the dance, the needle, cards.
But Miss *Weichmann's* mind needs things more recondite,
To comfort and appease her innate drive to write,
Than trifles such as cards, the needle, and the dance.
And if she wants to play, she weaves her own garlands,
With Pierian laurel leaves, as fitting for her head,
And climbs up Mt. Parnassus to pass the time instead.
If I see this lively step, then I think I can
Say she is not *Weich* ("soft"), but really is Miss *Mann*.

WANTING TO ANSWER MR. DARNMANN'S UNDESERVED
CIVILITY IN THE SAME RHYME-SCHEME, I REMAIN, HIS
OBEDIENT SERVANT, H. E. WEICHMANN

What miracle is this! what! I should blush, I know it!
Does Mr. *Darnmann* deign to count me as a poet?
So be it! In his lively verses he asserts politely, oh!
That I could join their ranks, perhaps e'en rightly so.
However, I myself do know and know my meager gifts.
And though I feel that poetry and music can uplift,
I wouldn't dare participate myself in poets' rounds,
And thus I willingly bequeath the stately laurel crowns
To the Pierians, those shrewd muses of antiquity.
I think that Mt. Parnassus looks too dangerous for me.
Seeing his gentility, I am thus forced to say,
That even poets are allowed to have their joke this way.

—S.L. *Cocalis*

MEINE JUGEND WAR GEDRÜCKT VON SORGEN

Meine Jugend war gedrückt von Sorgen,
Seufzend sang an manchem Sommermorgen
Meine Einfalt ihr gestammelt Lied;
Nicht dem Jüngling thöneten Gesänge,
Nein, dem Gott, der auf der Menschen Menge,
Wie auf Ameishaufen niedersieht!
Ohne Regung, die ich oft beschreibe,
Ohne Zärtlichkeit ward ich zum Weibe,
Ward zur Mutter, wie im wilden Krieg,
Unverliebt ein Mädchen werden müßte,
Die ein Krieger halb gezwungen küßte,
Der die Mauer einer Stadt erstieg.

BRIEF AN MARIANA ZIEGLER

Wenn uns das Manns-Volk höhnt, ich ziehe gleich vom Leder,
Wenn der und jener spricht: Ihr schlechten Tauben ihr,
Wie hoch verfliegt ihr euch, was nehmen Weiber für;
Wenn mancher Pinsel sagt, wir pflegten nachzumahlen,
So will ich mich bemühn, die Tadler zu bezahlen. [. . .]
Frau! Weltberühmte Frau, der Eifer nimmt mich ein,
Auf, laß diß frevle Volck nicht sonder Straffe seyn.
Zeigt sich kein scharffer Stahl an unsern tapffern Seiten,
So laß uns diesen Schwarm mit unserm Kiel bestreiten.

ANNA LOUISA KARSCH (1722–1791)

MY YOUNG DAYS WERE OPPRESSED WITH CARES

My young days were oppressed with cares,
On summer mornings I sat there,
Sighing my poor stammered song.
Not for a young man was my melody,
No! for God who the crowds of men does see
As if they were an anthill's throng.
Without emotions, as I've often said,
Without affection, I was wed,
Became a mother, as in times of war
A young girl would not trust love's bliss,
On whom a soldier forced his kiss,
Whose army reigned as conqueror.

—*S.L. Cocalis*

ANNA HELENA VOLCKMANN (c. 1736)

LETTER TO MARIANA ZIEGLER

When men-folk scoff at us, I have to draw my sword,
When this or that one says: You naughty pigeons, you!
You're flying much too high, what are you trying to do?
When some cretin says, we've no creative mind,
Then I will be sure to pay him back in kind. [. . .]
Woman! world-famed woman, with ardor I'm aflame,
Don't let this wanton sex get off without the blame.
And even if we don't have sharp blades like the men,
Still let us fight this pack with our sharpened pen.

—*S.L. Cocalis*

DER KUß IM TRAUME

Es hat ein Kuß mir Leben eingehaucht,
Gestillet meines Busens tiefstes Schmachten.
Komm, Dunkelheit! mich traulich zu umnachten,
Daß neue Wonne meine Lippe saugt.

In Träume war solch Leben eingetaucht,
Drum leb' ich, ewig Träume zu betrachten,
Kann aller andern Freuden Glanz verachten,
Weil nur die Nacht so süßen Balsam haucht.

Der Tag ist karg an liebesüßen Wonnen,
Es schmerzt mich seines Lichtes eitles Prangen
Und mich verzehren seiner Sonne Gluthen.

Drum birg dich Aug' dem Glanze irrd'scher Sonnen!
Hüll' dich in Nacht, sie stillet dein Verlangen
Und heilt den Schmerz, wie Lethes kühle Fluthen.

AN CREUZER

Seh' ich das Spätroth, o Freund, tiefer erröthen im Westen,
Ernsthaft lächelnd, voll Wehmuth lächelnd und traurig verglimmen,
O dann muß ich es fragen, warum es so trüb wird und dunkel,
Aber es schweiget und weint perlenden Thau auf mich nieder.

KAROLINE VON GÜNDERODE (1780–1806)

THE DREAM KISS

A kiss once breathed life into me,
Stilled deepest longing in my breast.
Come, darkness! come with your caress,
That my lips may suckle blissfully.

Such life was there immersed in dreams,
So I live to contemplate them ceaselessly,
The other joys' allures mean naught to me,
Since only night exhales sweet balsam streams.

The day is sparing with lovely sweet delights,
The light's vain glitter hurts my eyes,
And the ardor of the sun consumes me.

Eye, take shelter from the luster of such earthly lights!
Wrap yourself in night, she will still your cries,
And heal the pain, like the cool, deep waves of Lethe.

—*S.L. Cocalis*

TO CREUZER

When I see the evening reds, friend, blushing deep in the west,
Smiling gravely, wistfully smiling and dying away,
Oh, then I must ask why it is so dim and so dark out,
But it is silent and cries pearling dew down upon me.

—*S.L. Cocalis*

AM TURME

Ich steh auf hohem Balkone am Turm,
Umstrichen vom schreienden Stare,
Und laß gleich einer Mänade den Sturm
Mir wühlen im flatternden Haare;
O wilder Geselle, o toller Fant,
Ich möchte dich kräftig umschlingen,
Und, Sehne an Sehne, zwei Schritte vom Rand
Auf Tod und Leben dann ringen!

Und drunten seh ich am Strand, so frisch
Wie spielende Doggen, die Wellen
Sich tummeln rings mit Geklaff und Gezisch
Und glänzende Flocken schnellen.
O, springen möcht ich hinein alsbald,
Recht in die tobende Meute,
Und jagen durch den korallenen Wald
Das Walroß, die lustige Beute!

Und drüben seh ich ein Wimpel wehn
So keck wie eine Standarte,
Seh auf und nieder den Kiel sich drehn
Von meiner luftigen Warte;
O, sitzen möcht ich im kämpfenden Schiff,
Das Steuerruder ergreifen
Und zischend über das brandende Riff
Wie eine Seemöwe streifen.

Wär ich ein Jäger auf freier Flur,
Ein Stück nur von einem Soldaten,
Wär ich ein Mann doch mindestens nur,
So würde der Himmel mir raten;
Nun muß ich sitzen so fein und klar,
Gleich einem artigen Kinde,
Und darf nur heimlich lösen mein Haar
Und lassen es flattern im Winde!

ANNETTE VON DROSTE-HÜLSHOFF (1797–1848)

ON THE TOWER

I stand on the tower's high balcony,
The shrieking starling streaks by.
And like a maenad I let the storm
Rumple and tear at my hair.
Oh my wild comrade and crazy boy,
I long to embrace you and match
My strength against yours, two steps from the edge
And wrestle with you to the death.

And as I look down at the beach, the waves
Are like hunting dogs at play,
Foaming and bellowing they rave,
And up leaps the glistening spray.
How gladly I'd jump to be among
That raging pack of hounds
And follow through the coral woods
The walrus with merry sound.

And further I see a pennant blow
Bold as a battle banner.
And the prow of the ship goes up and down,
As I watch from my airy rampart.
Oh, I want to stand in that fighting ship
And grasp the steering wheel
And over the spitting, hissing deep
Glide as the seagull will.

If I were a hunter, out in the wild,
If I were a bit of a soldier,
If I were at least and simply a man,
Then Heaven would counsel and hold me.
But now I must sit like a good little girl,
Sweet, delicate and fair.
And I have to hide to let the wind
Blow freely through my hair.

—*Ruth Angress*

DER KRANKE AAR

Am dürren Baum, im fetten Wiesengras
Ein Stier behaglich wiederkäut' den Fraß;
Auf niederm Ast ein wunder Adler saß,
Ein kranker Aar mit gebrochnen Schwingen.

»Steig auf, mein Vogel, in die blaue Luft,
Ich schau dir nach aus meinem Kräuterduft.«—
»Weh, weh, umsonst die Sonne ruft
Den kranken Aar mit gebrochnen Schwingen!«

»O Vogel, warst so stolz und freventlich
Und wolltest keine Fessel ewiglich!«—
»Weh, weh, zu viele über mich,
Und Adler all—brachen mir die Schwingen!«

»So flattre in dein Nest, vom Aste fort,
Dein Ächzen schier die Kräuter mir verdorrt.«—
»Weh, weh, kein Nest hab ich hinfort,
Verbannter Aar mit gebrochnen Schwingen!«

»O Vogel, wärst du eine Henne doch,
Dein Nestchen hättest du im Ofenloch.«—
»Weh, weh, viel lieber ein Adler noch,
Viel lieber ein Aar mit gebrochnen Schwingen!«

FARBENWECHSEL

Warum doch gehst du immer grau gekleidet?
So sprach der Freund zu einer ernsten Frau.
Mein Aug' sich gern an bunten Farben weidet,
Du aber gehst so lange schon in Grau.

Mein treuer Freund, dir will ich es wohl sagen,
Die graue Stimmung herrscht mir im Gemüth,
Und keine Schillerfarben kann ich tragen,
Seit mir des Lebens Baum hat abgeblüht.

THE AILING EAGLE

Near a lifeless stump in a fertile lea
A bull ruminated on its feed;
A wounded eagle sat low upon the tree,
An ailing bird with broken wings.

"Rise up, my bird, into the clear blue sky.
In my fragrant bed I'll watch you fly."
"Alas! Alas! In vain the sun does cry
To the ailing eagle with broken wings!"

"O bird, it's your wickedness and vanity
And lifelong scorn of all captivity!"
"Alas! Alas! too many above me—
And all eagles—broke my wings!"

"So, off the branch, flutter to your nest,
You'll ruin my herbs with your distress."
"Alas! Alas! I have no place to rest,
Exiled eagle with broken wings!"

"O bird, if only you were just a hen,
You could live in a stove vent"—
"Alas! Alas! I'd rather be an eagle, then,
Much rather be an eagle with broken wings!"

—*S.L. Cocalis and G.M. Geiger*

KATHINKA ZITZ-HALEIN (1801–1877)

CHANGE OF COLOR

Why do you always dress in gray?
A friend said to an earnest dame.
I love to see bright colors display'd
But you are always dressed the same.

I'd like to tell you, my dear friend,
A grayish mood controls my soul,
And I can't wear bright-colored blends,
Since I've felt myself grown old.

Das Kind trug Weiß—der Unschuld Engelfarbe
Umhüllte es so duftig, hell und klar,
Und aus der Ähren aufgehäufter Garbe
Zog es sich Blumen für sein Lockenhaar.

Dann kam die Zeit der aufgewachten Triebe
Die in dem Lenz des Lebens feurig glüh'n;
Ich ging im Kleid der rosenrothen Liebe
Und in der Hoffnung heilig-schönem Grün.

Dann kam ein Tag, der brachte die Gewänder
Der wilden feuerfarbnen Leidenschaft,
Die mich umschloß mit ihren Glutenbänder,
Mir aufgezehrt des Geistes rege Kraft.

Die Gattin ging einher im blauen Kleide
Der ewig duldenden Ergebenheit,
Und später trug ich violette Seide,
Die Farbe die dem edeln Zorn geweiht.

Getragen hab' ich wohl auch Purpurgluten
Die tief empfundner Schmerz auf mich vererbt,
Denn ach! der Stoff, er war ja in den Fluten
Aus meines Herzens bestem Blut gefärbt.

Dann sah ich Jahre auf mich nieder schweben
Wie Rabenzüge mit dem Unglücks-Flug,
In welchen ich um ein verfehltes Leben,
Das dunkle Schwarz der tiefen Trauer trug.

Allmählich trug ich Braun—denn die Bestrebung
Des Selbstbewußtseins lichtete den Sinn.
Die braune Farbe deutet auf Ergebung
In ein Geschick an dem ich schuldlos bin.

Jetzt ist das Grau die Farbe meiner Tage,
Das Sinnbild einer blassen Dämmerzeit,
In der gestorben ist so Freud als Klage.
Die graue Farbe zeigt Gleichgültigkeit.

Gleichgültigkeit! —Hab' alles ich vergessen?
Begraben jedes Hochgefühl. —O nein!
Für's Vaterland, für große Zeitintressen
Wird nimmermehr mein Herz gleichgültig sein. [. . .]

The child wore white, angelic shade of innocence,
Which brightly enveloped the little girl.
And from the corn-sheaves' opulence
She crafted flowers for her golden curls.

Then came the time of awakening desire,
Which flared up, burned in life's new spring;
Love's rosy red I chose for my attire
And hope's lovely green for everything.

Then came a day with new costumes,
Which signified a wild and fiery passion.
By its ardent flames I was consumed,
My lively spirit spent and ashen.

The wife was clad in clothes of blue,
For lifelong suffering and devotion;
Later came silks of violet hue,
For noble anger and emotion.

I've also worn a glowing scarlet,
Which deep-felt pain did there impart;
For, alas, the cloth, it had been ret,
Dyed in the best blood of my heart.

Then I saw the years were passing by
Like flocks of ravens' ill-starred flight;
Then knowing how I'd failed in life, I
Donned widow's weeds, as black as night.

Gradually, I switched to brown—for the affirmation
Of my self-confidence did much to ease my mind.
The brown tones signified my resignation
To a fate that's been no fault of mine.

Now gray is the color of my days,
The twilight years it represents,
Where joy and grief have passed away.
For gray is the emblem of indifference.

Indifference!—Have I forgotten everything?
Buried all my joy—Oh no, indeed!
For my country and my king
My heart will never cease to beat. [. . .]

—S.L. Cocalis and G.M. Geiger

JEANNE MANON PHILIPON-ROLAND

Die heil'ge Lieb' zum Vaterlande,
Sie ist kein Hirngespinnst, kein Wahn,
Sie lebt und fachet ihre Flammen
Auch in dem Herz der Frauen an.
Das Rechte lehrt sie sie errathen,
Führt sie auf der Begeistrung Bahn,
Und zu der Höhe großer Thaten
Trägt sie ihr Schwindelflug hinan.

Dich, reich an Schönheit, Seelenadel,
Die hoch saß auf des Geistes Thron,
Dich riß in ihren wilden Strudel
Das Ungethüm Revolution.
Doch wolltest du nicht glänzen, blitzen,
Dich trieb nicht an die Eitelkeit,
Du wolltest deinem Volke nützen
In der Parteien wildem Streit.

Mit deinem Worte, mit der Feder,
Verfochtest du des Volkes Recht;
Hoch wie die Schwalbe in den Äther,
Hobst du dich über dein Geschlecht.
Du warst ein Mann in Frauenröcken,
Ein edler, kühner, freier Mann,
Und schloßest zu den besten Zwecken,
Dich an die Girondisten an.

Wie glänzte dein begeistert Auge,
Aus dem ein Heer von Funken schoß,
Wenn deinem feingeschnittnen Munde,
Der kühne Redestrom entfloß.
Die Massen hast du oft beweget
Mit deines Worts gewalt'ger Macht,
Und auch, wie wenn der Sturm sich leget,
Zur Ruhe wieder sie gebracht.

Doch als die Bergpartei jetzt siegte
Im Lauf der Dinge, die sich dreh'n,
Da war es um die Girondisten,
Da war es auch um dich gescheh'n.
In Banden wurdest du geschlagen
Und mußtest schon nach kurzer Frist,
Aus deinem dumpfen Kerker tragen
Dein schönes Haupt auf's Blutgerüst.

JEANNE MANON PHILIPON-ROLAND*

The sacred love for one's native land,
Is neither chimera nor whim,
It's real and can burst into flames,
Even in female limbs.
It teaches women what is right,
Fills them with enthusiasm,
And its dizzy, headstrong flight
Bears them to heights of heroism.

You, endowed with beauty, noble soul,
Who sat upon the spirit's throne,
You were swept into the whirlpool
Of that monstrous revolution.
But you did not want to star,
You were not moved by vanity:
You wished alone in this wild war
To combat inhumanity.

With your words and with your pen
You fought for human rights;
You rose above your fellow women,
Like a swallow taking flight.
You were a man in women's dress,
A noble, daring, and free man:
And with the noblest of intents,
You were a Girondist partisan.

How your inspired eyes did glow,
From which a host of sparks shot forth,
When from your finely chiseled mouth
A stream of daring words has poured.
You've often stirred up hordes of men
With the power of your eloquence,
And then you've calmed them down again,
Like a storm whose force is spent.

But as the Mountain Party triumphed
In the changing course of history,
The Girondists had had their day
And you had also seen your glory.
You were bound in iron chains
And shortly afterwards were told
To leave your musty cell again
And you were brought up to the scaffold.

*Marie-Jeanne Roland (1754–1793) was a Girondist during the French Revolution.

Du gingest stolz—dein Auge strahlte
Und deine Wangen waren roth,
Du hattest wie ein Mann gehandelt,
Und wie ein Mann gingst du zum Tod.
Um deines Volkes Heil zu stählen
Hast du geopfert Gut und Blut—
Du konntest in den Mitteln fehlen,
Allein dein edler Zweck war gut.

Der Gatte, dir in Lieb' ergeben,
Der treu dich hielt in seiner Brust,
Er konnte dich nicht überleben,
Zu schmerzlich war ihm dein Verlust.
Mit dir war all sein Glück entschwunden
Jetzt war er einsam und allein,
Da gab er sich die Todeswunden,
Um so mit dir vereint zu sein.

MEINE SPRACHE

Ich, ich sollt' armselig singen,
Wie's behagt der armen Welt,
Sollte *den* Ton lassen klingen,
Der ins Ohr ihr schmeichelnd fällt?
Sollte meinen Jammer schmücken,
Daß er ja voll Grazie sei,
Sollt' mit Anstand unterdrücken
Meines Busens Schmerzensschrei?

Nein, in solche Fesseln schmiede
Ich die freie Seele nicht!
Wär' für mich ein Trost im Liede,
Wenn der Mund, das Herz nie, spricht?
Fragt der Sturm und fragen Wellen,
Ob gefällt ihr mächt'ger Klang?
Fragt's der Vogel, wenn im hellen
Himmel schmettert froh sein Sang?

Proudly you went and your eyes were shining,
And your cheeks glowed bright red.
Like a brave man you had acted,
And like a man you met your death.
To protect the welfare of your race,
You sacrificed all that you had:
Although your path led to disgrace,
One cannot say your goal was bad.

Your husband, who loved you faithfully,
Remained devoted in his heart.
Your loss struck him so painfully,
He could not bear to see you part.
With you his happiness had gone,
And thus, one day he took his life,
After living lonely and alone,
To be reunited with his wife.

—*S.L. Cocalis and G.M. Geiger*

IDA HAHN-HAHN (1805–1880)

MY LANGUAGE

I, I should sing as wretchedly
As would suit the wretched world,
Should produce just that one sound
That is flattering to its ears?
Should embellish my misery,
So that it sounds charming,
Should suppress, as is proper,
The cry of pain in my breast?

No, in such fetters I'll
Not cast my free spirit!
Would a song afford me any consolation
That comes from the mouth and not the heart?
Do the storm and the waves ask
If their mighty sounds are pleasing?
Does the bird ask when its joyous song
Resounds in the bright sky?

»Wohl! in Weltenharmonien
Tönen sie nur unbewußt,
Wie ein Gott es hat verliehen!«
Wohnt kein Gott in meiner Brust?
Er, er hat mir ja gegeben
Voll Erbarmen jedes Lied,
Das durch mein so schaurig Leben
Wie ein Zaubersegen zieht.

Freundlich läßt es mich vergessen
Diese Erd' und ihre Qual.
Kann ich denn den Jubel messen,
Der mich hebt zum Göttermahl?
Und im Sturme der Gefühle
Bietet kühn das Wort sich dar,
Wie der Blumen bunt Gewühle
Eine Frühlingsnacht gebar.

Mag's als Dissonanz hier tönen;
Doch halt' ich am Glauben treu,
Daß in einer Welt des Schönen
Es kein harter Mißton sei
Darum red' ich meine Sprache!
Mag sie nie zum Herzen geh'n,
Wart' ich still und ohne Klage,
Droben wird man sie versteh'n.

DER WANDERVOGEL

Es segelt ein Schiff auf dem tiefblauen Meer,
Ein glitzerndes Vögelchen flieget daher.

Es setzt auf dem Mast sich behaglich zur Ruh'
Und singet ein liebliches Liedchen dazu.

Da staunet das Schiffsvolk, denn plötzlich so leicht
Wird Mühe und Arbeit, und Sorge entweicht.

»Der Vogel kann zaubern! er strahlt in die Fern',
Bei Tag eine Sonne, zur Nachtzeit ein Stern!«

Mit einmal erhebt sich sein schimmernder Flug,
Verlassend das Schiff, das so freudig ihn trug.

"Indeed! In the harmony of the spheres
They will sound unconsciously,
As is a god's behest!"
Is there no god in my breast?
He, He it was, who's given me,
For He is merciful, that very song,
Which runs through my wretched life
Like a magic blessing.

Obligingly it allows me to forget
This earth and its afflictions.
Can I measure the elation
That elevates me to feast with the gods?
And in the storm of feelings
The word presents itself boldly,
Like a colorful patch of flowers
Born of a spring night.

Even if it sounds discordant here,
I still will cling to the belief
That in a world of Beauty
It will not be harshly dissonant.
Thus I'll speak in my language!
Even if it never reaches the heart,
I shall wait quietly and without complaint,
It will be understood up above.

—S.L. *Cocalis*

BIRD OF PASSAGE

  Upon the deep ocean a schooner is lying,
To it a small, glistening bird comes flying.

  It sits down to rest, settles down on the mast,
And sings a sweet ditty when some time has passed.

  The ship's crew must marvel, for as the bird sings,
Their toil, their work, and their cares take to wing.

  "The bird's a magician! it shines from afar,
By day it's a new sun, by night it's a star!"

  At once, rising up in its shimmering flight,
It takes leave of the ship that has shown such delight.

»Du falsch-falscher Vogel, o bleibe doch hier,
Du bringst uns ja Glück und verleihest uns Zier.«

»Ade, du mein Schiffchen, du selbst bist nicht treu!
Du ziehest dahin und daher und vorbei.

So mach deinen Weg! ich erwart' dich im Port,
Und singe unsterbliche Lieder dir dort.«

ROSANE

*(Zwischen Landeck und Flirsch in Tyrol, wo sich
der wilde Bergstrom, die Rosane, wie
in Verzweiflung durch's enge Thal stürzt.)*

»Hast Du einmal mich verloren,
»Bringt mich keine Macht zurück—«
Spricht Rosane, und verschwindet
Vor des Berggeists bangem Blick.

Treu ist er ihr nicht gewesen,
Schaut 'ne Andre liebend an,
Und Rosane stürzt verzweifelnd
Auf die wilde Felsenbahn.

Er gebietet allen Quellen,
Allen Bächen ihren Lauf:
»Stürzet Euch zu ihr hernieder,
»Haltet die Rosane auf.—«

Und sie rieseln, fließen, stürzen,
Wie der Bergesfürst gebot;
Doch Rosanens mächt'ger Wille
Lockt sie in den frühen Tod.

»Wähnt nicht, Thoren, mich zu halten,
»Nimmer kehr' ich heimatwärts!
»Glücklichen mögt ihr gebieten,—
»Frei geht durch die Welt der Schmerz.«

"You false-hearted bird, oh, please won't you stay!
You bring us good fortune, adorn our pale day."

"Adieu, my dear ship, it is you who's untrue!
You go off to this place, to that one, you do.

So be on your way! when you land before long,
I will be there and sing you my immortal song."

—S.L. Cocalis

ROSANE

*(Between Landeck and Flirsch in Tyrol, where the wild
torrent, the Rosane, throws herself precipitously through
the narrow valley, as if in despair.)*

"After you have lost me once,
I'll be gone for all your days"
Rosane says and disappears
Before the Berggeist's* anxious gaze.

He has not been true to her,
He looks with longing at some Miss,
And, desperate, Rosane hurls
Herself over the precipice.

He rules over all the waters,
Tells them where to take their course:
"Now plunge down after her,
And hold Rosane back by force."

And they ripple, flow, plunge downwards,
As the Berggeist bid his slaves.
But Rosane's mighty will
Just lures them to an early grave.

"Fools, don't think you will restrain me,
You will never see that day!
You may rule the fortunate,
But grief is free to find its way."

—S.L. Cocalis

*The Berggeist is the spirit ruling the mountain and the waters there.

DEN FRAUEN

Ihr richtet streng, der Sitte heil'ge Fehm,
Und schleudert auf mein Haupt das Anathem!
Mögt ihr zu Boden stürzen eure Kerzen
Und schlagen an die Brust, so tugendreich:
Ich fühl' es mächtig in dem tiefsten Herzen,
Daß meine Sünde eurer Tugend gleich'.

Der Unschuld Lilien mögen euch umblühn,
Das Roth der Schaam auf euern Wangen glühn;
Wie Schwäne sich auf stillen Fluthen schaukeln,
Gefühle still durch eure Seele ziehn;
Wie Falter neckend durch die Blumen gaukeln,
Der Liebe Wünsche leis' vorüberfliehn!

Quält euch ein Flammen Sehnen fessellos,
Mögt ihr entsagen stolz und seelengroß;
Mögt still verzehren eure heiße Jugend,
Auskämpfen ritterlich den heil'gen Krieg,
Und mit dem Vollmachtsbriefe eurer Tugend
Dem Tod, der Hölle nehmen ihren Sieg!

Ich achte dennoch eure Tugend nicht,
Verwerfe kühn eu'r heiliges Gericht!
Seid des Gesetzes Hort, der Sitte Rächer,
Des frommen Glaubens treuer Genius!
Es lebt ein heil'ger Geist auch im *Verbrecher*.
Der Freie sündigt, weil er sünd'gen muß!

Das Leben auch verlangt sein mächtig Recht,
Verläßt des starren Wortes todten Knecht;
Aus edlem Feuer flossen meine Sünden,
Aus Drang des Herzens, glüh'nder Leidenschaft.
Für sie würd' ich schon hier Vergebung finden,
Die Zeugen meines Werthes, meiner Kraft.

Entsagen ist der Nonne Stolz und Ruhm,
Beglücken ist des Weibes Heiligthum,
Ihr wollt mühsam die Ewigkeit ergründen,
Mir lächelt sie aus jedem Augenblick;
Ihr wollt das Glück in eurer Tugend finden,
Ich finde meine Tugend nur im Glück.

LOUISE ASTON (1814–1871)

FOR WOMEN

You judge severely moral values, Fehme,*
And at my head you hurl your anathema!
May you throw your candles to the ground
And beat your breasts, you who are so virtuous:
I feel it strongly in my heart, deep down,
That my sins and your virtues are synonymous.

Chastity's lilies may bloom all around you,
And with modesty your cheeks change hue;
And emotions, like swans gliding on still water,
May pass through your souls so quietly;
And love's wishes, like butterflies who flutter
Teasingly among the flowers, flee by gently.

Should an unfettered, ardent passion cause you pain,
You may renounce it proudly, with disdain;
May let it eat you up inside,
Gallantly waging battle in this sacred war,
And death and hell are thus denied
With this proof of goodness, virtue's guarantor!

Nevertheless, your virtues I cannot respect,
And your sacred, moral court I must reject!
Avenge moral transgression, be the refuge of the laws,
And the guardian angel of the faith that you profess!
A holy spirit is also found in the *outlaw*.
The free man sins, because he must transgress!

Life also claims its due, making strong demands,
And leaves behind dead servants of the Covenant;
My sins resulted from a noble flame within,
From burning passion, the throbbing of my breast.
Even here I could find forgiveness for my sins,
Which to my strength and value do attest.

Renunciation is the pride and glory of a nun,
To delight is the sacred task of woman;
You strive unceasingly to find eternity,
I see it smiling in each day's caress;
You want to find true happiness in chastity,
I find my virtue in happiness.

*Secret imperial court of justice in Westphalia until 1808.

Wenn mich der Liebe Flammen heiß umsprühn,
Will ich in sel'gem Feuertod verglühn;
Doch aus den Gluthen steig' ich neugeboren,
Wie sich der Phönix aus der Asche schwingt,
Geläutert ward mein Wesen—nicht verloren,
Zu neuem, heil'gem Liebesglück verjüngt.

LIED EINER SCHLESISCHEN WEBERIN

Wenn's in den Bergen rastet,
Der Mühlbach stärker rauscht,
Der Mond in stummer Klage
Durch's stille Strohdach lauscht;
Wenn trüb die Lampe flackert
Im Winkel auf den Schrein:
Dann fallen meine Hände
Müd in den Schooß hinein.

So hab' ich oft gesessen
Bis in die tiefe Nacht,
Geträumt mit offnen Augen,
Weiß nicht, was ich gedacht;
Doch immer heißer fielen
Die Thränen auf die Händ'—
Gedacht mag ich wohl haben:
Hat's Elend gar kein End?

Gestorben ist mein Vater,
Vor Kurzem war's ein Jahr—
Wie sanft und selig schlief er
Auf seiner Todtenbahr'!
Der Liebste nahm die Büchse,
Zu helfen in der Noth;
Nicht wieder ist er kommen,
Der Förster schoß ihn todt.

Es sagen oft die Leute:
»Du bist so jung und schön,
Und doch so bleich und traurig
Sollst du in Schmerz vergehn?«
»Nicht bleich und auch nicht traurig!«

When I am surrounded by love's crackling fire,
I want to burn to ashes on a sacred pyre;
Yet from the glowing embers I am born again,
And rise up like the phoenix from the dust:
My soul's been purified—it has not been condemned,
I have become young again for love's sacred trust.

—*S.L. Cocalis*

SONG OF A SILESIAN WEAVER

When the hills are resting calmly,
One hears the rushing brook,
The moon in silent protest
Shines through the thatched roof;
When the lamp flickers dimly
In the corner on the chest:
Then my hands sink wearily
Into my lap to rest.

So have I often sat there
And as the darkness grew,
I dreamt with my eyes open,
But of what, I wish I knew.
Then hot and heavy fell
The tears upon my hands—
In my dream I asked myself:
Will this misery never end?

My father has been dead now
For just about a year.
How blissfully and softly
He slept upon his bier!
My loved one took a rifle
To try to keep us fed;
He never came back here again,
The warden shot him dead.

People often tell me:
"You are so young and fair,
And yet so pale and wretched,
You shall die of despair!"
"I'm neither pale nor wretched!"

Wie spricht sich das geschwind
Wo an dem weiten Himmel
Kein Sternlein mehr ich find'!

Der Fabrikant ist kommen,
Sagt mir: »mein Herzenskind,
Wohl weiß ich, wie die Deinen
In Noth und Kummer sind;
Drum willst Du bei mir ruhen
Der Nächte drei und vier,
Sieh' dieses blanke Goldstück!
Sogleich gehört es Dir!«

Ich wußt' nicht, was ich hörte—
Sei Himmel du gerecht
Und lasse mir mein Elend,
Nur mache mich nicht schlecht!
O lasse mich nicht sinken!
Fast halt' ich's nicht mehr aus,
Seh' ich die kranke Mutter
Und's Schwesterlein zu Haus'!

Jetzt ruh'n so still sie alle,
Verloschen ist das Licht,
Nur in der Brust das Wehe,
Die Thränen sind es nicht.
Kannst du, o Gott, nicht helfen,
So lass' uns lieber gehn,
Wo drunten tief im Thale
Die Trauerbirken steh'n!

EIN HEIL'GES FEST

O dieser Tag der höchsten Feier,
Der mir das Herz im Busen bricht;
Der höhnend durch der Zukunft Schleier
Mir zeigt des Schmerzes Angesicht!
Ein Schmerz, der nicht in leichtem Beben,
In flüchtigem Vorüberschweben
Die schwarze Trauerfahne trägt—
Nein, der ein ganzes, reiches Leben
Mit schonungsloser Hand zerschlägt!

One can say that easily,
While in the great, wide heavens,
There's not one star for me!

The factory owner came to me,
And said: "My dearest child,
I know full well your family's fate
Is anything but mild;
And so if you will stay with me
—Say, three or four nights long—
See this piece of shining gold!
To you it shall belong!"

I knew not what was happening—
Oh, heaven, pray be just
And leave me to my misery,
But don't think it was lust!
Oh, pray don't abandon me!
I can't go on much more:
When I see my poor, sick mother,
And my sister at the door!

Now they all are resting,
The light's gone out again.
My tears have ceased to flow,
And yet my plight remains.
Oh, God, if you can't help me,
You'd better let us go,
Down into the valley
Where the weeping willows grow.

—S.L. Cocalis and G.M. Geiger

A SACRED CEREMONY

Oh, this day of sacred rites,
Which will break my heart in two,
Which, while sneering, sheds its light,
Puts future suffering out on view!
A pain it is, that will not wear—
Just fleetingly, suspended in the air,
Just mildly trembling—the black mourning band—
No, into a thousand pieces will it tear
A whole, flowering life with its relentless hand.

Nicht ahnt's der Kranz in meinen Locken,
Daß ich dem Tode angetraut;
Nicht ahnen es die Kirchenglocken,
Zu läuten einer Grabesbraut!
Umsonst mit euern milden Tönen
Wollt ihr dem Leben mich versöhnen;
Mich lockt kein festlich heitrer Klang!
Nur meinen Schmerz kann er verhöhnen;
Nur feiern meinen Untergang!

Verkauft ein ganzes reiches Leben,
Das seines Werts sich kaum bewußt,
Mit Träumen, die das Herz durchbeben
In wilder, ahnungsvoller Lust!
Ein glühend Schwelgen, süßes Bangen,
Ein fiebrisch zitterndes Verlangen,
Das um das Glück gebietrisch fleht,
Bis von dem kalten Tod umfangen
Das Leben und der Traum verweht!

Du Herr der Welt, du Lebenswürger,
O falsches, gleißendes Metall!
Verlockst du selbst des Himmels Bürger,
Den stolzen *Geist*, zum Sündenfall?
Die sich nach ew'gen Himmeln sehnen,
Die kühn sich unvergänglich wähnen,
Verkaufen die ein ew'ges Sein.
Der Priester segnet Schmerz und Tränen,
Er segnet selbst den Meineid ein!

Erlöscht, ihr Kerzen am Altare!
Erlöscht wie meiner Seele Licht!
Das Brautbett wird zur Totenbahre,
Um die man Grabeskränze flicht.
Es tritt auf allen meinen Wegen
Verzweiflung spottend mir entgegen,
Mit irrem Blick, mit wildem Haar;
Verzweiflung sprach den Hochzeitsegen,
Sprach ihren Fluch am Traualtar!

Fluch diesem Tage höchster Feier,
Der mir das Herz im Busen bricht!
Der höhnend durch der Zukunft Schleier
Mir zeigt des Schmerzes Angesicht!

The wreath in my hair does not suspect,
That death is my real fiancé;
The church bells ringing don't detect
That for a bride of death they play!
Your mild tolling is in vain
If you want me to come to life again;
Your festive tones don't lure me!
You can only scorn my pain;
And celebrate that you can't cure me!

Sell out a whole flowering and abundant life,
Which hardly realized what it is,
With dreams that now the heart do rive,
With wildly foreshadowed bliss!
A sweet longing for the revel's fire,
A feverish, trembling, warm desire,
That, commanding, begs for happiness,
Until cold death forces to expire
Both life and dream in its caress.

You, Lord of the world, you, life-destroying one,
Oh you, falsely shimmering material!
Would you tempt heaven's proudest son,
The noble intellect, to sin, to fall?
Those who long for life eternal,
Who boldly think they are immortal,
Are they selling an eternal life?
The priest who blesses pain and tears shall
Bless an act of perjury: such is this sacred rite!

Go out, you candles on the altar!
Go out like the flame of my own soul!
The wedding chamber is the burial vault,
For which funeral wreaths cannot console.
Wherever I may choose to go,
Despair its mocking face does show,
With raving eyes and wild brows;
Despair, the wedding blessing did bestow,
By cursing us after our vows!

A curse upon this day of sacred rites,
Which will break my heart in two!
Which, while sneering, sheds its light,
Puts future suffering out on view!

Ein Schmerz, der nicht in leichtem Beben,
In flüchtigem Vorüberschweben
Die schwarze Trauerfahne trägt—
Nein, der ein ganzes, reiches Leben
Mit schonungsloser Hand zerschlägt!

EINEM WELTLING

Fruchtlos hab' in Schmerzenstoben
Ich vor dir geweint, geras't;
Und die Welt, sie wird dich loben,
Daß du mich verlassen hast.

Rühmend wird sie zu dir sagen:
»Kluger Mann, der, stark und fest,
Durch gebrochner Seelen Klagen
Nimmer sich beirren läßt;«

»Dessen Wille gleich dem Pfeile
Rastlos fliegt zum Ziele fort,
Ob er auch in seiner Eile
Ein befreundet Herz durchbohrt!«

»Kluger Mann, der zum Beleid'gen
Solche Opfer sich erkürt,
Die zu rächen, zu vertheid'gen
Sich kein Mensch auf Erden rührt!«

»Kluger Mann, der alte Bande,
Wenn sie lästig werden, bricht!«
Sag! fühlst du die ew'ge Schande,
Die aus solchem Lobe spricht?

A pain it is that will not wear—
Just fleetingly, suspended in the air,
Just mildly trembling—the black mourning band—
No, into a thousand pieces will it tear
A whole, flowering life with its relentless hand.

—*S.L. Cocalis*

BETTY PAOLI (1814–1894)

TO A MAN OF THE WORLD

Before you I have cried in vain
And raved in throes of agony;
But you the world will not disdain,
Because you have abandoned me.

Approvingly to you they'll say:
"Shrewd man, how strong and stalwart,
Who never let himself be swayed
By sad laments of broken hearts.

"Whose will is like an arrow's flight,
Directed grimly at its goal,
Although a hasty oversight
May pierce some kindred soul!

"A clever man, no doubt, will find
Such victims to abuse,
Whom no one out of all mankind
Would defend, avenge, excuse!

"A clever man, no doubt, disclaims
Old ties when love abates!"
Tell me, don't you feel the blame
That such praise articulates?

—*S.L. Cocalis and G.M. Geiger*

AN GEORGE SAND

Du bist erhöht und in den Staub getreten,
Gekrönt mit Ruhm, gezeichnet mit Verhöhnung;
Für Tausende und dich ist nie Versöhnung,
Und dir zu nahen, würden sie erröthen.

Ich nahe dir—ich biete dir die Rechte,
Ich liebe dich und will es frei bekennen.
Nimm meine Hand zum Bund—nicht soll uns trennen,
Was ich an dir verlöscht, vergessen möchte.

Wenn du nicht bist wie wir, und nicht ertragen
Und lächeln willst, es ist nicht dein Verschulden;
Du kannst es nicht. Drum kämpfst du, wo wir dulden,
Und sprengst die Fesseln, die wir still ertragen.

Wohl hast du viel gefehlt in irrem Streben,
Hast manche Schranke frevelnd überschritten,
Die heilig ist; allein auch viel gelitten,
Und deinem Schmerze kann ich viel vergeben.

Doch Jene, die dich richten und verdammen,
Was wissen sie von dir und deinem Geiste?
Schlug in ihr Herz, das öde, das vereiste,
Ein Funken je von deines Herzens Flammen?

Durchreißt ihr Blick die Sonne, die sie blendet?
Verstehen sie, der Armuth bleiche Hüter,
Den Reichen wohl, der, stolz auf seine Güter,
In kühnem Uebermuth sie frei verschwendet?

Und hat ihr Herz aus Wunden je geblutet,
Wie tückisch sie verhüllte Feinde schlagen?
Und ist ihr Herz in todesdunkeln Tagen
Von namenlosen Thränen überflutet?

Gewiß, sie müssen, fest, in Einem Bunde,
Abwehren dich von ihrem kalten Leben,
Denn ihre Seele könnte ja erbeben
Von einem Liebeshauch aus deinem Munde.

IDA VON REINSBERG-DÜRINGSFELD (1815–1876)

TO GEORGE SAND

You've been both exalted and debased,
Crowned with glory, heaped with insults,
Thousands despise you as a result,
And they would blush to meet you face to face.

I approach you—offer you my hand,
I love you, admit it freely from my heart.
Accept my vow—let discord not keep us apart,
These conflicts from my thoughts are banned.

If you're not like us and will not suffer,
And smile nicely, stop, it is not your fault;
You cannot do it. You'd attack, where we'd default,
And loose the shackles that we'd mutely suffer.

Along your way you've erred, time and again,
You've wantonly overstepped your bound'ries,
Sacred bounds, alas, you've also suffered profoundly,
And I can forgive you, considering your pain.

But those who pass judgment and set blame,
What do they know of you or of your talent?
Were their barren, frozen hearts ever rent
By but a spark of your soul's raging flame?

Can they know the sun if blinded by its brilliance?
Can they understand, these poor guardians of poverty,
The rich man, who, proud of his gifts and property,
Squanders them freely in his dashing arrogance?

And has their heart ever bled from wounds
That were dealt maliciously and by cloaked foes?
And did their heart ever overflow
With nameless tears on death-dark afternoons?

Surely, they must join together, tightly, as they do
To shut you out of their heartless existence,
For their souls might shudder in your presence
Were they touched by a breath of love from you.

—*S.L. Cocalis and G.M. Geiger*

GESTÄNDNIS

Und weil ich schwieg und weil in keuscher Scheue
Ich nimmer auf dem offnen Markt gesungen,
Von meiner Seele ew'ger Liebestreue,
Von meines Herzens süßen Huldigungen:

Meint Ihr, ich sei kein fühlend Weib geblieben,
Indes der Freiheit Fahne ich getragen?
Ich hab' verlernt zu dulden und zu lieben,
Weil meine Lieder keine Liebesklagen?

O arme Thoren, die Ihr noch könnt wähnen,
Daß stille Lieb' und lautes Wort sich einen,
Daß wir die heiligsten von unsern Thränen
Vor aller Welt vermögen auszuweinen.

Hört Ihr die Nachtigall am Tage schlagen
In lauter Menschen emsigem Gewimmel?
Sie wird zur Nacht im stillen Haine klagen,
Den Menschen nicht, sie singt ihr Lied dem Himmel.

Die Lerche aber singt im Sonnenscheine,
Sie ruft die Menschen wach zu neuen Thaten.
Wo sie der Arbeit pflegen im Vereine,
Schwebt sie am liebsten ob den grünen Saaten.

So hab' ich Euch als Lerche aufgeweckt,
Das Morgenlied der Freiheit vorgesungen,
Als Nachtigall hab' ich mich tief verstecket—:
Das Lied der Liebe ist in Nacht verklungen!

FÜR ALLE

Für alle! hören wir die Worte tönen,
Da wird das Herz uns plötzlich groß und weit!
Sie künden uns wie mit Drommetendröhnen
Den Siegsgesang der echten Menschlichkeit.
Denn anders ist kein heilig' Werk zu krönen

LOUISE OTTO-PETERS (1819–1895)

CONFESSION

And since I was silent and lived in chaste timidity,
I never dared to sing out on the marketplace,
About the vows of life-long spiritual fidelity,
About the loves that my heart would embrace:

Do you think I had become insensitive
Because under freedom's flag I went?
That I had forgot to love and give
Because my songs weren't love laments?

O poor fools, that you can imply
That secret love be one with spoken words,
That we could bring ourselves to cry
Our most sacred tears so they be heard.

Can you discern the nightingale by day
Amid the bustling throng of people here?
At night in silent groves will she display
Her art to heavenly, not human ears.

The lark, however, sings by daylight,
She rouses people to perform new deeds.
She prefers to fly where men unite,
And work collectively over greening seeds.

Thus as a lark I have awakened you,
With morning songs of freedom's fight.
Like a nightingale I withdrew—:
The song of love has faded in the night.

—S.L. Cocalis and G.M. Geiger

FOR ALL

For all! We hear the words resound
And our bosoms swell up suddenly!
They announce to us like trumpet sounds
The triumphant song of true humanity.
For no sacred mission can be crowned,

Und anders nie zu enden Kampf und Streit,
Als wenn ein Heil, das in die Welt gekommen
Der Sonne gleich für alle ist entglommen.

»Für alle!« sangen einst der Engel Scharen
In jener gottgeweihten heil'gen Nacht,
»Für alle will der Herr sich offenbaren
In seiner ewigtreuen Liebesmacht;
Für alle hat er Noth und Tod befahren
Und der Erlösung großes Werk vollbracht,
Das gleich den Gliedern eines Leibes einte
Mit festem Band die gläubige Gemeinde.«

»Für alle—« klang es im Hussitenheere—
«Ist auch der Gnade Kelch mit Christi Blut,
Denn allen ward verkündet seine Lehre,
Die in der Gleichheit aller Menschen ruht,
Und Erd' und Himmel hat nicht höhre Ehre,
Als nun uns wird mit dem geweihten Gut.«
Im Märtyr'tum, in grauser Todeshalle
Ertönt es noch: »Der Kelch des Heils für alle!«

So wußten sie die Losung recht zu fassen,
Erteilten sie an Mann und Weib zugleich.
Sie wollten nicht das hohe Erbteil lassen,
Das Bürgertum im neuen Liebesreich.
Da gab es keinen Neid mehr und kein Hassen,
Kein Sklaventum, kein Herrschen stark und feig,
Die Seelen galt's, die freien, zu erretten
Aus düsterm Bann, aus schwerer Knechtschaft Ketten.

Wo wieder aber ward der Ruf vernommen:
»Für alle Freiheit!« klang es fast wie Hohn,
Denn für die Männer nur war er gekommen
Im Wettersturm der Revolution.
Denn schien auch Joch auf Joch hinweggenommen,
Und stürzte auch in Trümmer Thron um Thron:
Dem Männerrecht nur galt das neue Ringen,
Das Frauenrecht blieb in den alten Schlingen.

Wohl grüßten freie Männer sich als Brüder,
Nur Bürger gab es, nicht mehr Herr und Knecht;
Wohl sangen sie der Liebe Bundeslieder
Und fühlten sich als ein erneut' Geschlecht.
Doch auf die Schwestern blickten stolz sie nieder,
Der Menschheit Hälfte blieb noch ohne Recht,
Blieb von dem Ruf: »für alle!« ausgenommen—
Ihr muß erst noch der Tag des Rechtes kommen.

And there can be no peace or amity,
Unless material prosperity, like the sun,
Would shine its healing rays on everyone.

"For all!" the host of angels pealed
On that sacred, holy night.
"For all, the Lord will be revealed
In His eternal, loving might.
For all, He suffered grave ordeals,
So we could see dear heaven's light.
Like all the members of one body, His demise
United all believers with firm ties."

"For all!"—the Hussite troops exclaimed—
"The blood of Christ brings immortality;
For all, His teachings were proclaimed,
Which profess the tenet of equality;
And the highest honor we on Earth may claim
Is His sacred consubstantiality."
In martyrdom, within a cruel death's halls,
It still resounds: "The sacred chalice is for all!"

Thus they recognized the Word's significance
And applied this sense to both sexes equally.
They didn't want to lose their proud inheritance,
The bourgeoisie in this realm of love and harmony.
There they knew no envy and no arrogance,
No slavery, no reigning strong and cravenly,
To deliver all free souls, this was their campaign,
To lead them out of darkness, to loose them from their chains.

The next time, however, that the cry was heard:
"Freedom for all!" it offered no serious solution,
Because on men alone rights were conferred
In the upheavals of the revolution.
For even though it seemed like changes had occurred
And like the monarchy was on the brink of dissolution:
Those new struggles were for the rights of man;
The rights of woman were not part of their plan.

The free men spoke of fraternization:
They were citizens, not lords and slaves;
They sang of their new affiliation
And considered themselves a reborn race.
But they viewed their sisters with deprecation—
There were no rights for half the populace,
For the cry "for all!" excluded women—
They were denied the rights of citizens.

Der Frauen Schar, die in den Staub getreten,
Ward nur erhoben an des Glaubens Hand.
Die Besten lernten fromm zum Himmel beten,
Weil ja die Erdenwelt sie nicht verstand;
Die andern aber ließen sich bereden
Sie seien nur bestimmt zu Spiel und Tand,
Es sei ihr höchstes Ziel im süßen Minnen,
Des ganzen Lebens Inhalt zu gewinnen.

Doch wiederum wird einst der Ruf erklingen:
So wie vor Gott sind wir auf Erden gleich!
Die ganze Menschheit wird empor sich ringen
Zu gründen ein erneutes Liebesreich,
Dem Weibe wie dem Mann sein Recht zu bringen
Zu wahren mit des Friedens Palmenzweig.
In laut'rer Wahrheit stolzem Siegesschalle
Tönt's noch einmal: »Erlösung kam für alle!«

SANKT PETER UND DER BLAUSTRUMPF

Ein Weiblein klopft an's Himmelsthor,
Sankt Peter öffnet, guckt hervor:
—»Wer bist denn du?«—»Ein Strumpf, o Herr...«
Sie stockt, und milde mahnet er:
»Mein Kind, erkläre dich genauer,
Was für ein Strumpf?« »Vergieb—ein blauer.«
Er aber grollt: »Man trifft die Sorte
Nicht häufig hier an unsrer Pforte.
Seid samt und sonders freie Geister,
Der Teufel ist gar oft nicht dreister,
Geh hin! er dürfte von dir wissen,
Der liebe Herrgott kann dich missen.«
—»Das glaub ich wohl—doch ich nicht Ihn,
O Heilger, wolle noch verziehn!«
Sie wagt es, sein Gewand zu fassen,

A host of women, who had been humiliated,
Could only rise up by God's hand.
The best turned to prayer and supplicated,
Because the world simply didn't understand.
The others, however, were persuaded
That they were born as playmates for a man,
That their highest goal and life's vocation
Were to tend to love's sweet ministration.

In time again, we'll hear this exclamation:
And as in heaven, here there'll be equality!
All human beings will strive for amelioration,
To found a realm of love and harmony,
Where both sexes share the rights of the nation
And preserve them with the palm branch of tranquility.
In the proud procession of the truth the call
Will ring out again: "Emancipation came for all!"

—*S.L. Cocalis and G.M. Geiger*

MARIE VON EBNER-ESCHENBACH (1830–1916)

SAINT PETER AND THE BLUESTOCKING

A woman knocks on the pearly gates
St. Peter opens, hesitates:
—"And who are you?"—"A stocking, sir..."
She falters and he gently chides her:
"My child, speak up and have you done!
What sort of stocking?" "Oh, a blue one."
He growls: "One would not anticipate
Meeting your sort at our gate.
You're all freethinkers, your whole crew,
Satan himself's no match for you.
Go to him! he knows you well
God won't miss you down in hell!"
—"I realize that—but it's Him I need,
Oh, please forgive me, please take heed!"
She dared to touch St. Peter's sleeve,

Hat auf die Knie sich sinken lassen:
»Du starker Hort, verstoß mich nicht,
Laß blicken mich in's Angesicht
Des Ewgen, den ich stets gesucht.«
—»In welcher Weise, ward gebucht;
Man strebt ihm nach, wie's vorgeschrieben,
Du bist uns fern und fremd geblieben.«
Das Weib blickt flehend zu ihm auf:
»Wär' Dir bekannt mein Lebenslauf,
Du wüßtest, daß in sel'gen Stunden
Ich meinen Herrn und Gott gefunden.«
Der Pförtner stutzt: »Allwo?—Sprich klar!«
—»Daselbst, wo ich zu Hause war,
(Mein Handwerk brachte das mit sich)
Im Menschenherzen. Wunderlich
War dort der Höchste wohl umgeben;
Oft blieb von Seines Lichtes Weben
Ein glimmend Fünklein übrig nur,
Und führte doch auf Gottes Spur.
Ob er sich nun auf dem Altare
Den Frommen reicher offenbare—
Das zu entscheiden ist Dein Amt.
Bin ich erlöst? bin ich verdammt?«
Sankt Peter zu derselben Frist
Etwas verlegen worden ist,
Dacht' eine gute Weile nach,
Nahm endlich doch das Wort. Er sprach
Und rückt dabei den Heil'genschein:
»Besprich es drin.—Ich lass' Dich ein.«

Supplicating, on her knees:
"Strong protector, do not look askance,
Let me see the countenance
Of the Lord I've always sought."
—"But have you done so as you ought?
One has to seek Him as we say
But you're a sheep who's gone astray."
On her knees, she supplicates:
"If only you could know my fate,
You'd know of the times profound
When my Lord and God I'd found."
The porter faltered: "Where? Speak up! Come!"
—"Where I lived, in my own home—
(That was part of my trade)
In the human heart. There I found displayed
The Almighty in His resting place;
Often, His light almost effaced,
Only a faint glimmer did prevail,
Yet this was enough to find God's trail.
Or does He reveal Himself solely
On your altars to the Holy?
To judge me now is your task:
Am I damned or saved, I ask."
St. Peter, as this was being said,
Felt his cheeks were turning red.
He thought it over for a while
And finally told her without guile
As he straightened up his halo:
"Ask in there.—There, in you go!"

—S.L. Cocalis and G.M. Geiger

SAPPHO

Ist's auch nur dein Name allein, der glorreich
Weithin durch Jahrtausende herrlich leuchtet,
Mit der Menschheit schaffenden Geistes-Helden
Ewig verbunden,

Hat das immergrüne Gerank der Sage
Auch so reich umschlungen dein Erdendasein,
Daß des Antheils forschender Blick es niemals
Könnte durchdringen—

Dennoch sei begeistert und freudig dankbar
Hoch gepriesen, du, deren edle Stirne
Schmückt der einz'ge Kranz, der uns hebt zu Göttern,
Jener des Genius!

Ja—du schufst das Lied! an die ersten Töne
Feurig—zart, da inneres Leben kündet
Auf des Wohllauts Schwingen die gold'ne Lyra—
Knüpft sich dein Name!

Ja, du schufst allein aus dir selbst, o Sappho!
Während tief barbarische, dumpfe Erdnacht
Später viel Jahrhunderte lang so trostlos
Hüllte die Menschheit,

Daß das unterjochte Geschlecht der Frauen
Kaum begriff, wie schmälich es drückt die Kette,
Während jetzt, da lange schon rings es Tag ward,
Tausende nimmer

Das Geschlecht zu trennen gelernt vom Geiste—
Strahlt aus fernsten Zeiten dein Name siegreich
Uns entgegen, hehr wie das ew'ge Sternlicht—
Sei uns gepriesen!

MARIE VON NAJMÁJER (1844–1904)

SAPPHO

Though only your name still shines
Across the millennia in glorious triumph,
Linked forever with the creative heroes of the spirit
Of humankind,

And the evergreen tendrils of legend
Have entwined about you so thickly
That the most avid of seekers after you
Cannot disentangle it,

Nevertheless be glad, and rejoice,
Exalted one, you whose noble forehead
Is graced with the only garland that makes us gods,
The garland of genius!

Yes, you created song! the first tones
Ardent, gentle, the golden lyre revealing
Your inner life in the melodic rhythms
Evoking your name!

Yes, you created from within yourself, O Sappho!
Though since then a barbaric dark age
Enveloped for so many centuries
Disconsolate humanity

That the oppressed female sex
Hardly realized how degrading its chains.
Yet even now, long after its beginning,
When thousands have still

Not learned to separate their spirit from their sex,
Still your name gleams
Like eternal starlight from faroff times—
Glory be unto you!

—*S.L. Cocalis and G.M. Geiger*

EIN MODERNES WEIB

Ein Mann beleidigte ein Weib. Es war
Von jenen schnöden Thaten eine, die
Kein Weib vergessen und vergeben kann.

Geraume Zeit verstrich. Da eines Abends
Ward an die Thür des Frevlers laut gepocht.
Er rief: »Herein«, und sah voll tiefen Staunens,
In Trauerkleidern eine Frau vor sich.

Sie schlug den Schleier bald zurück. Er blickte
In ihre großen stolzerstarrten Augen,
In diese großen schmerzversengten Augen...
Er lächelte verlegen, denn ein Schauer
Erfaßte ihn...Er bot ihr höflich Platz,
Sie aber dankte, und mit ruhiger Stimme
Sprach sie zu ihm: »Du hast mich schwer beleidigt,
Es war nur Gott dabei...vor diesem Gott,
Vor dir, und mir allein, will ich den Flecken
Den Makel meiner Ehre, zugefügt
Von deiner Hand, verlöschen.
                                    Höre nun!
Um dies zu thun, bleibt mir ein Mittel nur:
Ich kann nicht gehn, um einem fremden Menschen
Das was ich selbst mir kaum zu sagen wage,
Zu offenbaren. Für mich herrscht kein Richter,
Er wär' denn blind und taub und stumm, deshalb
(Ein Schildern des Vergangenen glich'aufs Haar
Der neuen That, hieß' selber mich entehren),
Deshalb gibt's eins nur: hier sind Waffen, wähle!«
Sie stellte auf den Tisch ein Kästchen hin
Und öffnete den Deckel.———
                                    Lange standen
Die beiden Menschen stumm. Er sah sie an,
Sie hielt das glänzend große Aug' gerichtet
Fest auf die Waffen.
                              Plötzlich brach er aus
In lautes Lachen. Da durchglühte feurig
Ein tiefes Rot die farbenlosen Wangen
Der jungen Frau. Wie, wenn die ganze Antwort
Dies Lachen wär'? Sie hätte schreien mögen
Vor Wut und Elend. Aber sie bezwang sich,

MARIE JANITSCHEK (1859–1927)

A MODERN WOMAN

A man had wronged a woman. It was
One of those despicable deeds that
No woman can forgive or can forget.

Some time elapsed. Then one evening
There came a knock. The culprit
Called: "Come in," and saw, to his surprise,
A woman in mourning before him.

She threw back her veil. He looked
Into her eyes, benumbed with pride,
Into those large eyes, seared with pain...
He laughed self-consciously, a shiver
Chilled his spine...He offered her a seat,
But she declined, and in a calm, firm voice
She said to him: "You have wronged me,
As God was my witness...and before this God,
Yourself, and myself alone, I want to clear
This stain on my honor for which
You are responsible.
                          Now listen!
To do this there is but one choice for me:
I cannot go and tell a perfect stranger
Things which I can hardly tell myself.
I could not recognize a judge except one
Blind and deaf and dumb. Therefore (if
I say what happened, where would that
Leave me? I would disgrace myself!), therefore,
There's no choice: here are weapons, choose!"
She placed a little box upon the table,
Opened up the lid.———
                          For a while
Both stood silently. He looked at her,
Her large and shining eyes were fixed
Upon the weapons.
                          Suddenly he broke out
Into peals of laughter. Then there glowed a fiery
Deep red in the pallid cheeks
Of the young woman. What if his only answer
Were this laughter? And she felt like screaming out
In anger and distress. But she controlled herself

Und sagte mild: »Wenn dir ein Unvorsichtiger
Zufällig auf den Fuß getreten wäre,
Du würdest ohne lange Ueberlegung
Ihm deine Karte in das Antlitz schleudern,
Nichts Lächerliches fändest du dabei.
Nun denk': nicht auf den Fuß trat mir ein Mensch,
Mein Herz trat er in Stücke, meine Ehre!
Verlang' ich mehr, als du verlangen würdest
Für einen unvorsichtigen Schritt, sag' selbst,
Ist das nicht billig?«
                              Lächelnd sah er ihr
Ins zornerglühte Antlitz. »Liebes Kind,
Du scheinst es zu vergessen, daß ein Weib
Sich nimmer schlagen kann mit einem Manne.
Entweder geh zum Richter, liebes Kind,
Gesteh ihm alles, gerne unterwerfe
Ich seinem Urteil mich. Nicht? Nun dann bleibt
Dir nur das eine noch: vergesse, was du
Beleidigung und Schmach nennst. Siehst du, Liebe,
Das Weib ist da zum Dulden und Vergeben...«
Jetzt lachte sie.
                              »Entweder Selbstentehrung
Wenn nicht, ein ruhiges Tragen seiner Schmach,
Und das, das ist die Antwort, die ein Mann
In unserer hellen Zeit zu geben wagt
Der Frau, die er beleidigt.«
                                        »Eine andere
Wär' gegen den Brauch.«
                                        »So wisse, daß das Weib
Gewachsen ist im neunzehnten Jahrhundert,«
Sprach sie mit großem Aug', und schoß ihn nieder.

And calmly said: "If some careless person
Had stepped upon your toe by chance,
You would—without thinking twice—
Throw your card into his face and
That wouldn't be a laughing matter.
Just think: no one's stepped on me,
My heart is trod upon, my honor!
Am I demanding more than you would
For a careless step? now you tell me
If that's not fair."
                        Smiling, he looked
Into her angry, glowing face. "Dear child,
You seem to forget that women
Cannot ask for satisfaction.
Either you go to a judge, dear child,
Confess all this to him and I will gladly
Heed his judgment. No? Then you will
Simply have to forget this so-called
Shame and insult. You see, my dear,
A woman suffers and forgives..."
Now she laughed.
                        "Either self-disgrace
Or if not, a silent sufferance of abuse,
And that, that's the answer that a man
In our enlightened times may dare to give
To her, the woman he has wronged."
                                "Society
Does not provide another."
                        "Then learn, that women
Change, have grown, this is the nineteenth century,"
She said, eyes opened wide, and shot him dead.

—S.L. Cocalis and G.M. Geiger

WIR FRAUEN

Das ist der Mond, der Blüte bringt
und in der Blüte tief die Frucht—
das ist der Mond, der Sonne trinkt
und Lieder jauchzt und Klarheit sucht.
Sie nannten ihn den Wonnemond,
und Kirschenblüten hat's geschneit...
wir aber feiern klaren Blicks
den Sonnentag des Völkerglücks,
den Blütenmond der neuen Zeit.

Wir feiern. Die wir rechtelos
—ein tiefgeknechtetes Geschlecht—
hindämmern in der Heimat Schoß,
wir feiern unser Bürgerrecht.
Wir hegen in der Mutterhut
der Zukunft lichten Maientrost;
wir halten in der Frauenhand
der Völkerfreiheit Unterpfand...
und rauschend geht der Wind aus Ost.

Wir feiern diesen Maientag:
denn laut an unserm Herzen klingt
des Mannesherzens Widerschlag,
der um das Heil der Menschheit ringt.
Wir feiern dieses Frühlingsfest:
wenn tief in unserm Schoße sprießt
die Hoffnung, die den Sieg empfängt,
die Sehnsucht, die zum Lichte drängt,
die Saat, die hoch in Halme schießt.

So feiern wir den ersten Mai,
der blütenstrotzend zieht ins Land:
wir stehn dem Mann im Kampfe bei,
gehn lachend mit ihm Hand in Hand.
Wir nahmen längst das stolze Recht,
das stumpfe Blindheit uns versagt...
der Lenz ist da! Die Zeit der Not
versinkt. Wir kämpfen—heiß und rot
der Freiheit Maienmorgen tagt.

KLARA MÜLLER-JAHNKE (1860–1905)

WE WOMEN

The spring moon it is that brings the buds
and the fruit that lies inside—
the spring moon it is that drinks in the sun
and, with songs of joy, seeks light.
They called it once the moon of bliss
and cherry blossoms fell like snow . . .
but we observe with clarity
the Sunday of prosperity,
the spring moon of a new epoch.

We celebrate. We, the oppressed,
—a sex always held subordinate—
kept dozing on our mother's breast,
our civil rights we celebrate.
In our maternal womb we hide
the promise of the coming spring;
and we hold in woman's hand
the pledge of freedom for our land,
which the eastern wind will bring.

We celebrate the first of May:
because upon our breasts we find
the hearts of men beating away—
they fight for us and all mankind.
We celebrate this holiday:
as we feel, deep in our womb,
the new hope that conceives our fight,
the longing to attain the light,
the seed that will burst into bloom.

Thus we celebrate the first of May,
which brings the blossoms to our land:
we join our men out in the fray,
go laughing with them, hand in hand.
We've taken back our rights
that years of blindness had withdrawn.
The spring is here! Hard times have fled.
We're fighting now—as hot and red,
the May day of our freedom dawns.

—S.L. Cocalis

DAS WAHLRECHT HER!

In der Arbeit mächt'gen Kreis
Sind wir längst hineingerissen.
Unsrer flinken Hände Fleiß
Kann die Erde nicht mehr missen.
Bei des Hammers hartem Schlag,
Bei dem Sausen der Maschinen
Mühen wir uns Tag für Tag,
Nur das Brot uns zu verdienen.

Was das Leben wert uns macht,
Wird zermürbt in dem Getriebe,
Frauenglück und Leidenschaft,
Selbst die heil'ge Mutterliebe.
Wie wir nur so nebenbei
Unsre Wirtschaft noch besorgen,
Geht das Leben uns vorbei
In dem Kampf um Heut und Morgen.

Karg der Lohn, voll Hohn das Wort,
Wenn wir Recht zu fordern wagen:
Schweigt! Die Küche ist der Ort,
Wo ihr rechtlos euch sollt plagen!
Darbt die Steuern euch vom Mund,
Die auf Salz und Brot gefallen,
Ringt euch Hand und Seele wund,
Denn wir ändern nichts von allem.

Doch aus unsrer großen Not,
Ward' uns heilger Zorn geboren,
Unsrer Kinder Schrei nach Brot
Klingt uns gellend in den Ohren.
Müssen wir nicht oft genug
Die Familie ganz ernähren?
Und doch will man uns den Zug
In die Parlamente wehren!

Wie so mancher alte Brauch
Mußte zeitgemäß sich wandeln!
Glaubt's, die Frauen lassen auch
Sich nicht mehr als Kind behandeln.

EMMA DÖLTZ (1866–1950)

GIVE US THE RIGHT TO VOTE!

For some time now we have been drawn
Into the force of working men.
The world would notice if we're gone,
Would miss our labor power then.
While the hammers bang away,
And engines roar full-speed ahead,
We labor, toil, day by day,
Just to earn our daily bread.

The things we value in this life
Are lost in this commotion:
The joys of love, of being wife,
And even motherly devotion.
As we try to run our households
In the time that we have free
We must watch our life unfold
Struggling with adversity.

Low the wages, words so base,
If we dare demand our rights:
Hush! The kitchen is the place
Where you should labor day and night!
Starve yourselves to pay the tax
That we have placed on salt and bread!
Wring your hands and break your backs,
We will not change things, as we've said.

Yet from our agonizing sighs
Was born our anger, sacred, fierce.
And our children's hungry cries
Echo shrilly in our ears.
Must we not, often enough,
Keep our families afloat?
Yet they constantly rebuff
Our moves to govern or to vote.

But like so many customs old,
With the times this must change too.
Believe me, we'll not be consoled,
Like the child-women you once knew.

Mit dem Spruch von Herr und Knecht
Habt ihr uns genug bestohlen.
Heut verlangt die Frau ihr Recht,
Und sie wird sich's mutig holen.

DIE HEIMARBEITERIN

Nur schnell die Augen ausgewischt,
Herr Gott, da hat's schon fünf geschlagen;
Wie kurz die Nacht, wie müd ich bin,
An allen Gliedern wie zerschlagen.
Schnell Feuer in den kalten Raum,
Das Frühstücksbrot noch schnell besorgen,
Damit man nur zum Nähen kommt,
Denn liefern, liefern muß ich morgen.

Dann eilt der Mann zur Arbeit hin,
Die Kinder nach der Schule gehen,
Und jedes braucht die Mutterhand,
Da heißt's jetzt doppelt fleißig nähen.
Bald kommt das Jüngste angekräht;
Bald heißt's den Mittagtisch besorgen,
Drum fleißig, fleißig nur genäht,
Denn liefern, liefern muß ich morgen.

So geht es weiter jeden Tag
In überstürztem, tollen Hasten,
Bis abends spät das brenn'de Aug'
Gebieterisch verlangt ein Rasten;
So werden Blut und Nerven schlecht
In der Gewohnheit dumpfer Schwere,
Und manchmal nur, bin ich allein,
Erkenn' ich bang des Herzens Leere.

Und dennoch ist nicht tot mein Sinn,
Und Stolz läßt hoch das Herz mir schlagen:
Daß mich die Kunst noch so ergreift,
Wie einst in meinen Jugendtagen.

Sie neigt sich liebevoll zu mir:
»Zu dir, zu dir bin ich gekommen!
Laß alles andre hinter dir,
Ich hab' dich jetzt ans Herz genommen.

You men have put us in this plight
With your master-slave decree,
But now we want to have our rights
And we shall gain them valiantly.

—*S.L. Cocalis and G.M. Geiger*

THE PIECE WORKER

Get up, now quickly wipe your eyes,
My God, the clock's struck five already;
How short the night, how tired am I,
My body's wracked, my hands unsteady.
Quick, the chilly room needs fire,
And quick, go fetch some breakfast bread;
So that you finally get to sew:
Tomorrow's quota must be met.

Off to work my husband rushes,
Off to school the children go,
And each one needs a mother's touches:
Nimbly, quickly I must sew.
But soon the youngest will come crying;
Then the lunch I'll have to get,
So keep that needle flying, flying,
Tomorrow's quota must be met.

And so it goes, day after day,
In frantic, crazy breathlessness,
Till late at night my burning eyes
Refuse to work, demand a rest.
My nerves and blood go bad this way,
This stifling dullness of routine,
And only rarely, when alone,
I see how empty life has been.

And yet my senses are not dead,
And yet my heart still swells with pride;
For art still moves me now as deeply
As when I was a simple bride.

Thus art approaches tenderly:
''I have come to you, to you!
It's you I've taken to my heart,
So bid all else adieu.

Und gehst du von mir, will ich dir
Den Schatz noch der Erinnrung geben,
Aus deines Alltags Einerlei
Will ich dir Herz und Sinn erheben,
Damit du Mann und Kindern kannst
Ein mutig, frohes Auge zeigen.
Drum hoch den Kopf! Vergiß es nicht:
Wer mich empfindet, bleibt mein eigen.«

DIE PUPPE

Liebe Puppe,
Wohlfrisierte kleine Puppe,
Wie hast du es leicht!
Du wendest das Köpfchen
Nach rechts und nach links,
Du lächelst, du schmollst,
Du weinst, du lächelst,
Und wenn man dich aufzieht
Am Knopf des Gefühlchens,
Des einzigen kleinen
Dir eignen Gefühlchens:
Der Liebe zu dir,
Zu dir, kleine Puppe,
So tänzelst du zierlich
Und neigst dich dankend
Dem Schwarm deiner Freunde,
Und äugst unter seidnen
Gebogenen Wimpern,
Ob du ihn nicht siehst,
Den schmerzlich ersehnten,
Ergebenen Diener,
Der an dem Knöpfchen
Des einen Gefühlchens
Dich liebevoll aufzieht
Bis an dein Ende,
Dein Puppenende....
Wir aber, entartet

And should you go, I'll give
You treasures for your memory,
I'll elevate your heart and mind,
Relieve you from monotony,
So that your husband, children see
How bravely, cheerfully you shine.
So lift your head! and don't forget:
Whoever knows me will be mine!''

—*S.L. Cocalis and G.M. Geiger*

MARGARETE BEUTLER (1876–1949)

THE DOLL

Dear doll,
Beautifully coiffed little doll,
How easy things are for you!
You turn your little head
To the right and to the left,
You smile, you pout,
You cry, you smile,
And when one winds up
The spring of your little feelings,
Of the only little feelings
That are yours:
Of love for you,
For you, little doll,
So you dance daintily
And curtsey, say thank you
To the crowd of your friends,
And look out from those silky,
Curling lashes,
Whether he might be there,
Whom you painfully long for,
Your devoted servant,
Who lovingly winds you
Up by the spring
Of your one little feeling,
Till death do you part,
Your doll's death . . .
But we, degenerate

Und vielfach geschmäht,
Wir andern, wir Ernsten,
Wir Dunklen, wir Schweren,
Wir Trägerinnen
Geheimen Wissen
Wir Deuterinnen
Uralter Runen,
Wir keuchen und brechen
Fast unter der Last
Des gnädigen Schicksals,
Das sie uns gab,
Unsre sehende Seele,
Von der du nichts weißt.—
O liebe Puppe,
Wohlfrisierte kleine Puppe,
Wie hast du es leicht!

DIE KOMMENDEN

Ein Kinderplatz, mit Sand und Ruß bedeckt,
von kläglich blassen Sträuchern eingeheckt.

Da wächst es auf, das kommende Geschlecht,
das einst—vielleicht!—der Mutter Thränen rächt.

Dort baut es ahnend sich ein hartes Ziel—
das Leben reicht ihm Steine überviel—

Und—es ist närrisch—ob dem Geisterbau
des Himmels zärtlichstes Septemberblau.

Von jener breiten Kinderstirne spricht
ein schwarzes Trotzen: Und ich weiche nicht.

Ich weiß schon längst, was in der Welt so Brauch,
und wie es Vater macht, so mach' ich's auch.

Mein Haß den Fetten an die Gurgel springt,
bis einst auch mich der blutige Strom verschlingt.

Dies Mädchen—wie ihr keck die Zunge geht—
sie sprach wohl nie ein Kindernachtgebet—

Noch trägt sie unbewußt ihr Lumpenkleid,
wie lange noch, dann kommt auch ihre Zeit.

And often abused,
We, the other women, the serious,
The dark, and the burdened,
We, who bear
Secret knowledge,
We, who interpret
Ancient runes,
We are gasping and straining
Under the weight
Of the merciful fate
That she gave us,
Our prophetic soul,
Of which you know nothing.—
O sweet doll,
Beautifully coiffed little doll,
How easy things are for you!

—S.L. Cocalis and G.M. Geiger

FUTURE GENERATIONS

Under a layer of soot and sand—a playground,
with pale and wretched shrubbery all around.

The future generations grow up here,
who will someday—perhaps—avenge their mothers' tears.

They set themselves a hard task there—
and life puts stones in their path everywhere.

Above this ghostly edifice—strange but true—
the heavens' most gentle autumn blue.

That broadbrowed child's face bespeaks
a dark defiance: and I don't retreat.

You bet, I know what people do
and my father's way is my way too.

I'll go kill fat cats ruthlessly,
until the blood-stream catches up with me.

This girl—oh, how her tongue runs wild—
could not have prayed much as a child.

She still—unconsciously—has on her tattered frock,
but soon she too will be summoned by the clock.

Dann schlingt sie schmutzige Bänder sich ins Haar
und bietet lachend ihre Reize dar.

Und ein paar Jahre roher Lust—dann hat
der Tod sie lieb auf sündiger Lagerstatt....

Wie dieser Knabenmund so schmerzlich ist!
Ach, wenn ihn niemand als der Hunger küßt!

Die Mutter wusch, bis sie zum Tode krank,
und als sie starb, da sprach sie: Gott sei Dank!

Ein altes Weib erstand den Knaben sich,
doch sie ist arm und hart und wunderlich.

Für ein Stück Brot in Morgennebelstund
läuft er sich Tag für Tag die Füße wund.

Und Tag für Tag saugt von den Lippen ihm
den Frühlingssegen seines Cherubim.

Sein Engel schläft—und Engel schlafen fest.
Kein Kinderjammer, der sie wachen läßt.——

Wie wildes, fruchtlos starres Binsenrohr,
wächst so Geschlecht hier für Geschlecht empor.

Und jeder Mai entlockt dasselbe Laub
den magern Sträuchern—blaß bedeckt mit Staub.

Weit, weit davon predigt die Sonnenpracht:
Ich bin das Licht, das alle glücklich macht.

SELBSTGERICHT

Ich habe mit getötet
Jeden, der draußen fällt.
Ich habe mich selbst inmitten
Des Meeres von Blut gestellt.

Then she'll tie dirty ribbons in her hair,
and offer her charms, laughing, everywhere.

And a few years of carnal lust—then death she'll meet:
they will know each other between her sinful sheets.

Oh, how tormented, painful, this little lad's mouth is!
What if it is only touched by hunger's kiss?

The mother took in wash, till she could walk no more,
and when she died, she said: "Praise the Lord!"

An old woman bought herself the child,
but she is eccentric, poor, not mild.

For a piece of bread in the morning-gray,
he runs his feet off every day.

And every day draws from him,
the spring blessing of his cherubim.

His angel sleeps—and angels' sleep is sound,
no child's misery can keep them around.

Like wild, stiffly barren needs,
each new generation grows and leaves.

And each May draws the same old green
Out from the meager shrubs, so ashen lacking sheen.

Far, far away the sunbeams might profess
to be the light that brings all happiness.

—*S.L. Cocalis and G.M. Geiger*

BERTA LASK (1878–1967)

SELF-JUDGMENT

I have helped to kill
Each man who dies, it's clear.
I have placed myself amidst
The sea of blood, I fear.

Mein Wille hat nicht zerbrochen
Kanone und Panzer und Schiff,
Hat nicht als ruhlose Welle
Ueberbrandet der Bosheit Riff.

Ich habe mich müd' und träge
Dem Willen der Menge geneigt,
Ob auch ein helles Glühen
Den Weg mir zum Leben gezeigt.

Meiner Seele auflodernde Flamme
Hab' ich feig bedeckt und gedämpft.
Ich habe nicht Stunde um Stunde
Für Wahrheit und Geist gekämpft,

Habe schweigend Unrecht ertragen
Und schweigend Unrecht getan,
Habe keinen Felsblock geschleudert
Gegen Mammons Kraft und Wahn.

Ich habe des Weibes Wissen
Aus Scheu vor der Mannmacht erstickt,
Meine blanken, geweihten Schwerter
Verborgen und nicht gezückt.

Da haben plötzlich die Schwerter
Sich eignes Leben errafft
Und würgen in Höhlen und Sümpfen
Meines Bruders Geist und Kraft.

So hab' ich aus Leib und Seele
Den Moloch Vernichtung gezeugt
Mit dir und dir und euch Allen,
Die gleich mir sich schlafselig gebeugt.

Wir haben mit getötet
Jeden, der draußen fällt.
Wir haben uns selbst inmitten
Des Meeres von Blut gestellt.

My will has not demolished
Cannon, and man-o-war, tank,
Nor has it like a restless wave
Submerged the reef of rancor.

I have made the will of the crowd
My own—wearily and lazily—
Although a brightly burning light
Showed the way of life to me.

The blazing flame that is my soul
I have sought to hide and soothe.
I have not fought for hours on end
For the spirit or for truth,

Silently I have suffered injustice
And silently I have been unjust,
Have not hurled any boulders
Against Mammon's madness and its thrust.

I have stifled woman's wisdom
In my awe of the power of men;
I have kept my shining, sacred swords
Concealed, and failed to brandish them.

But a life of their own
The swords took on
And in caves and swamps they slay
My brother's brain and brawn.

Thus from my body and soul I've begotten
The Moloch of extermination
With you and you and all of you,
Who, like me, have borne subjugation.

We have helped to kill
Each man who dies, it's clear.
We have placed ourselves amidst
The sea of blood, I fear.

—S.L Cocalis and G.M. Geiger

DIE JÜDISCHEN MÄDCHEN

*Die jüdischen Mädchen einer kleinen polnischen Ortschaft stürzten
sich, nachdem sie von den eingefallenen Russen vergewaltigt
worden waren, ins Wasser.*

Mit dem Gesicht gegen die Mauer
Liegt die kleine Channe in Krampf und Schauer.
Mitten in der Stube auf dem Boden sitzt Esther.
Sie sieht nicht mehr auf die kleine Schwester.
Ein Tuch ist vor das Fenster gehängt,
Und zwischen Tuch und Holzrand zwängt
Sich vom blauen Himmel ein Streifen.
Auf den starrt Esther mit dunklen, reifen
Augen, mit Augen fragend und groß.
Ihre Hände lösen sich im Schoß.
Ihre Blicke bleiben in den Streifen stehen.
Sie sinnt, hat sie dies helle Blau schon gesehen?
Als sie draußen ging mit ihren Schwestern,
Vor tausend Jahren oder gestern?
Es ist anders, es ist so neu.
Sie sieht es mit Augen schauernd und scheu.—
Die Türe geht auf. Gehüllt in dichte Falten
Kommen zwei Mädchen, die sich an Händen halten.
Sie treten vor Esther und blicken scheu zur Erde
Und klagen mit stummer Gebärde.
Und Esther nickt.—Und andre Mädchen kommen herein,
Manche mit Schluchzen und Schrein,
Manche schäumend vor Haß und Zorn,
Manche starr wie im Traum verlorn.
Eine dunkle, blitzäugige schreit:
»Wir schleichen ihnen nach. Sie sind nicht weit.
»Wir werfen Bomben auf ihre Schienen,
»Legen in ihre Quartiere Minen.
»Ich werde Gift mischen in ihre Speisen.
»Ich will sehn, wie ihre Blicke brechen und vereisen.«
Sie wirft sich hin und schlägt mit den Fäusten die Dielen.
Esther beugt sich nieder, ihre Stirn zu kühlen.
Die Anderen stehen wartend um sie her.
Sie sitzt auf dem Boden groß, ernst und schwer.
Mit dem Gesicht gegen die Mauer
Zuckt die kleine Channe in Krampf und Schauer.
Esther sieht in den Streifen Licht
Und spricht:
»Wir haben einst von Gott eine Seele bekommen.

THE JEWISH GIRLS

*The Jewish girls of a small Polish community flung
themselves into the water after they had been raped
by the invading Russians.*

With her face to the wall
Little Channe lies in convulsions.
Esther is sitting on the floor in the middle of the room.
She doesn't look at her little sister any more.
Cloth has been draped over the window
And between the cloth and the wooden frame
A sliver of blue sky squeezes in.
Esther stares at this with dark, mature
Eyes, with large, questioning eyes.
Her hands go limp in her lap.
Her gaze remains bound by the sliver of sky.
She wonders: has she ever seen this light blue before?
When she was out for a walk with her sisters
A thousand years ago or yesterday?
It is different, it is so new.
She views it with awed and startled eyes.—
The door opens. Swathed in thick wraps,
Two girls enter, holding hands.
They walk up to Esther, their eyes averted shyly,
And lament with silent gestures.
And Esther nods.—And other girls come in,
Some sobbing and crying,
Some seething with hate and rage,
Some benumbed, as if lost in revery,
A dark girl with flashing eyes screams:
"We'll sneak up on them. They aren't far away.
We'll throw bombs at their rails,
Place mines in their quarters.
I'll poison their food.
I want to see how their eyes dim and glass over."
She flings herself down and pounds the floor with her fists.
Esther bends down to cool her forehead.
The others stand waiting around her.
She is sitting on the floor, large, serious and ponderous.
With her face to the wall,
Little Channe lies in convulsions.
Esther looks at the sliver of light
And speaks:
"Once we received a soul from God.

»Aber man hat uns genommen,
»Als wären wir eine tote Erdmasse,
»Durch die fremder Wille sich reißt eine Gasse,
»Eine Gasse, drin zu wühlen und zu treten—
»Und läßt sie dann liegen.—Da hilft kein Beten.«
Esther schweigt fragend. Aber alle sind still.
Alle horchen, was Esther will.
Nur eine zitternde Stimme sagt: »Ich bin ganz leer.
»Esther, ich habe keine Seele mehr.«
Esther lächelt weh mit hellem Gesicht
Und spricht:
»Die Seele, die wir von Gott in uns tragen,
»Können Menschen nicht zertreten und zerschlagen.
»Aber sie will sich vor Scham verstecken,
»Denn ihre Hülle hat häßliche Flecken.
»Ich weiß nicht, warum das ist und kam.
»Aber unsre Seele versteckt sich voll Scham.
»Wir wollen nicht, daß unsre Seelen sich verstecken.
»Unsre Seelen sollen sich stolz hochrecken.
»Wir wollen nicht, daß sie weinend am Boden liegen.
»Unsre Seelen sollen jauchzen und auffliegen.
»Wer hilft unsren Seelen von ihrem Weh?
»Wir müssen reinwaschen die Hüllen draußen im See.«
Esther nimmt von der Bank das zuckende Kind
Und drückt es an sich fest und lind.
An ihre Wange preßt sie das kleine Gesicht,
Aber anschauen kann sie es nicht.—
Und als sie kamen ans dunkle Wasser,
Da wurde Manche noch stiller und blasser.
Esther sieht Klein-Channe ins Gesicht.
Es ist, als ob etwas in ihr zerbricht.
Und Esther spricht:
»Vater, wir bitten Dich, laß unser Leben
»Weiter über dem Wasser hier schweben.
»Mir ist so angst, daß wir ganz vergehn,
»Und Klein-Channe kann Sonne und Wald nie mehr sehn.
»Wir sind so jung, und wir sterben nicht gern.
»Und Du bist so hoch und bist so fern.
»Wenn Du kannst, nimm uns in Dich hinein!
»Mach uns leicht und hell! Sieh, wir waschen uns rein.«

Und dann sind sie ins Wasser gegangen.
Mit den Armen hielten sie sich umfangen.

But we have been taken
As if we were a dead piece of earth,
Through which strangers can pave a street at will,
A street that they can dig up and trample—
And then abandon.—Prayer can't help us there."
Esther falls silent and waits. But all are quiet.
They are waiting to hear what Esther says.
Only one trembling voice says: "I'm completely empty,
Esther, I don't have a soul anymore."
Esther smiles woefully with a luminous countenance
And speaks:
"The soul that we have received from God
Cannot be trampled and shattered by men.
But it wants to hide with shame
Since its mortal frame has ugly stains.
I don't know why that is and came to be.
But our souls are hiding with shame.
We don't want our souls to hide.
Our souls should swell with pride.
We don't want them to lie on the ground, crying.
Our souls should rejoice and soar.
Who will help our souls in their affliction?
We must cleanse our mortal frames out in the lake."
Esther takes the convulsive child from the bench
And hugs her gently, firmly.
She presses the little face to her cheek
But she can't look at her.—
And as they came to the dark water,
Some of them became more silent and paler.
Esther looks into little Channe's eyes.
It is as if something is broken in her.
And Esther speaks:
"Father, we beg You to let our lives
Hover over the water here.
I'm so afraid that we'll vanish entirely
And that little Channe will never see the sun or forest again.
We're so young and we don't want to die.
And You are so high and far away.
If You can, take us up unto You!
Make us light and clear! Look, we are cleansing ourselves."

And then they went into the water.
They clung to each other as they went.

—S.L. Cocalis

DIE GEMALTE MADONNA SPRICHT

Was tat er mir? Ich weiß nicht mehr, wer ich bin.
Ein dichter Nebel umlagerte meinen Sinn.
Was träufelte langsam in mein Hirn und Herz?
Es tat nicht weh und war doch wie tiefer Schmerz.
Einst war ich ein Mädchen und schritt durch Sonne und Sturm,
Nun bin ich in Linien und Farben gebannt wie in Ketten und Turm.

Was tat er mir? Hat er all mein Menschsein verzehrt?
Ich sitze gekrönt auf Wolken und lächle verklärt.
Die Menschen blicken anbetend verzückt zu mir hin.
Mir aber ist arm und trotzig und traurig zu Sinn.

Wie schön war eignes Schreiten in wehender Luft.
Er hat mich begraben in seines Traumes Gruft.
Nun bin ich erstarrt in meinen Farben und meinem Glanz.
Und draußen wirbelt jauchzend des Lebens Tanz.

DIE DICHTERIN

Du hältst mich in den Händen ganz und gar.

Mein Herz wie eines kleinen Vogels schlägt
In deiner Faust. Der du dies liest, gib acht;
Denn sieh, du blätterst einen Menschen um.
Doch ist es dir aus Pappe nur gemacht,

Aus Druckpapier und Leim, so bleibt es stumm
Und trifft dich nicht mit seinem großen Blick,
Der aus den schwarzen Zeichen suchend schaut,
Und ist ein Ding und hat ein Dinggeschick.

Und ward verschleiert doch gleich einer Braut,
Und ward geschmückt, daß du es lieben magst,
Und bittet schüchtern, daß du deinen Sinn
Aus Gleichmut und Gewöhnung einmal jagst,

THE PAINTED MADONNA SPEAKS

What has he done to me? I don't know what's become of me.
A heavy fog has enveloped me.
What has seeped into my heart and brain?
It didn't hurt and yet I felt it as a sharp pain.
Once I was a girl and strode through sun and gale.
Now I've been fixed in painted lines, as if in chains and jail.

What has he done to me? Has he consumed my humanity?
Crowned, I sit on clouds and smile beatifically.
People look up to me, worshipping, enrapt.
Yet I feel so wretched, sullen, trapped.

How nice it was to walk and feel the breeze.
He has buried me in the tomb of his reveries.
In my luster and my color, I am petrified
And outside, the dance of life triumphantly whirls by.

—*S.L. Cocalis*

GERTRUD KOLMAR (1894–1943?)

THE WOMAN POET

You hold me now completely in your hands.

My heart beats like a frightened little bird's
Against your palm. Take heed! You do not think
A person lives within the page you thumb.
To you this book is paper, cloth, and ink,

Some binding thread and glue, and thus is dumb,
And cannot touch you (though the gaze be great
That seeks you from the printed marks inside),
And is an object with an object's fate.

And yet it has been veiled like a bride,
Adorned with gems, made ready to be loved,
Who asks you bashfully to change your mind,
To wake yourself, and feel, and to be moved.

Und bebt und weiß und flüstert vor sich hin:
»Dies wird nicht sein.« Und nickt dir lächelnd zu.
Wer sollte hoffen, wenn nicht eine Frau?
Ihr ganzes Treiben ist ein einzig: »Du...«

Mit schwarzen Blumen, mit gemalter Brau,
Mit Silberketten, Seiden, blaubesternt.
Sie wußte manches Schönere als Kind
Und hat das schönre andre Wort verlernt.—

Der Mann ist soviel klüger, als wir sind.
In seinem Reden unterhält er sich
Mit Tod und Frühling, Eisenwerk und Zeit;
Ich sage: »Du ..« und immer: »Du und ich.«

Und dieses Buch ist eines Mädchens Kleid,
Das reich und rot sein mag und ärmlich fahl,
Und immer unter liebem Finger nur
Zerknittern dulden will, Befleckung, Mal.

So steh, ich, weisend, was mir widerfuhr;
Denn harte Lauge hat es wohl gebleicht,
Doch keine hat es gänzlich ausgespült.
So ruf ich dich. Mein Ruf ist dünn und leicht.

Du hörst, was spricht. Vernimmst du auch, was fühlt?

DIE UNERSCHLOSSENE

Auch ich bin ein Weltteil.
Ich habe nie erreichte Berge, Buschland undurchdrungen,
Teichbucht, Stromdelta, salzleckende Küstenzungen,
Höhle, drin riesiges Kriechtier dunkelgrün funkt,
Binnenmeer, das mit apfelsingelber Qualle prunkt.

Meiner Brüste Knospen spülte nicht Regen,
Kein Strahl riß sie auf: diese Gärten sind abgelegen.
Kein Abenteurer hat noch meiner Wüstentäler goldenen Sand besiegt
Und den Schnee, der auf hohen Öden jungfräulich liegt.

Nacktrote Felsgurgel würgen Kondore mit kralligen Fingern,
Spreiten die Federmäntel in Lüfte und ahnen nichts von Bezwingern.
Sind Adler? Auch Urweltadler—wer lauschte, wenn einer schrie?—

But still she trembles, whispering to the wind:
"This shall not be." And smiles as if she knew.
Yet she must hope. A woman always tries,
Her very life is but a single "You..."

With her black flowers and her painted eyes,
With silver chains and silks of spangled blue.
She knew more beauty when a child and free,
But now forgets the better words she knew.

A man is so much cleverer than we,
Conversing with himself of truth and lie,
Of death and spring and iron-work and time.
But I say "you" and always "you and I."

This book is but a girl's dress in rhyme,
Which can be rich and red, or poor and pale,
Which may be wrinkled, but with gentle hands,
And only may be torn by loving nails.

So then, to tell my story, here I stand.
The dress's tint, though bleached in bitter lye,
Has not all washed away. It still is real.
I call then with a thin, ethereal cry.

You hear me speak. But do you hear me feel?

—*Henry A. Smith*

WOMAN UNDISCOVERED

I too am a continent.
I have unexplored mountains, bushlands impenetrable and lost,
Bays, stream-deltas, salt-licking tongues of coast,
Caves where giant crawling beasts gleam dusky green,
And inland seas where lemon-yellow jellyfish are seen.

No rains have washed my budded breasts,
No springs burst forth from them: these gardens are remote from all
      the rest.
And no adventurer has claimed my desert valley's golden sands,
Or crossed the virgin snows atop my highest barren lands.

With taloned fingers condors strangle naked gullets of red stone,
Spread feathered coats in air, suspect no master, and abide alone.

Doch meine großen Geier sind mächtiger noch und fremder als sie.

Was ich hülle, bricht nie mehr aus schon erschlossenen Erden;
Denn dort leitet kein Schlangenwidder starr zuckende Vipernherden,
Leuchten durch Nächte nicht Kröten sich mit dem Karneol im Haupt.
Der Geheimnisse kupferner Kelch ward längst aus dem wehrenden
    Moos geklaubt.

Über mir sind oft Himmel mit schwarzen Gestirnen, bunten
    Gewittern,
In mir sind lappige, zackige Krater, die von zwingendem Glühen
    zittern;
Aber auch ein eisreiner Quell und die Glockenblume ist da, die ihn
    trinkt:
Ich bin ein Kontinent, der eines Tages stumm im Meere versinkt.

DIE KATZE

Die Katze, die einer fand, in der Baugrube saß sie und schrie.
Die erste Nacht, und die zweite, die dritte Nacht.
Das erste Mal ging er vorüber, dachte an nichts
Trug das Geschrei in den Ohren, fuhr auf aus dem Schlaf.
Das zweite Mal beugte er sich in die verschneite Grube
Lockte vergeblich den Schatten, der dort umherschlich.
Das dritte Mal sprang er hinunter, holte das Tier.
Nannte es Katze, weil ihm kein Name einfiel.
Und die Katze war bei ihm sieben Tage lang.
Ihr Pelz war gesträubt, ließ sich nicht glätten.
Wenn er heimkam, abends, sprang sie ihm auf die Brust, ohrfeigte
    ihn.
Der Nerv ihres linken Auges zuckte beständig.
Sie sprang auf den Vorhang im Korridor, krallte sich fest

Are eagles there, primordial? And who would hear if one would
  scream?
But my great vultures are more powerful than they, and stranger than
  a dream.

What I conceal will never break from cultivated soil;
For there no serpent rams lead herds of snakes that twitch and coil,
No toads shine through the night with reddish gems imbedded in
  their heads.
The copper chalice long ago was dug from clinging moss; its secrets
  are all dead.

Above me, often skies are black with stars or bright with
  thunderstorms;
Inside me flicker lobed and jagged craters filled with violent glowing
  forms;
But an ice-pure fountain I have as well, and the flower that drinks
  there quietly:
I am a continent that one day soon will sink without a sound into the
  sea.

—*Henry A. Smith*

MARIE LUISE KASCHNITZ (1901–1974)

THE CAT

The cat that someone found sat in a construction site and screamed.
The first night and the second and the third night.
The first time, passing by, not thinking of anything,
He carried the scream in his ears, heard it waking from a deep sleep.
The second time he bent down over the snow-covered ditch,
Trying in vain to coax out the shadow prowling around there.
The third time he jumped down, fetched the animal,
Called it cat, because no other name occurred to him.
And the cat stayed with him seven days.
Her fur stood on end, refused to be smoothed.
When he came home at night, she leapt on his chest, boxed his ears.
The nerve in her left eye twitched constantly.
She leapt up onto the curtains in the hall, dug in with her claws,

Schwang hin und her, daß die eisernen Ringe klirrten.
Alle Blumen, die er heimbrachte, fraß sie auf.
Sie stürzte die Vasen vom Tisch, zerfetzte die Blütenblätter.
Sie schlief nicht des Nachts, saß am Fuß seines Bettes
Sah ihn mit glühenden Augen an.
Nach einer Woche waren seine Gardinen zerfetzt
Seine Küche lag voll von Abfall. Er tat nichts mehr
Las nicht mehr, spielte nicht mehr Klavier
Der Nerv seines linken Auges zuckte beständig.
Er hatte ihr eine Kugel aus Silberpapier gemacht
Die sie lange geringschätzte. Aber am siebenten Tag
Legte sie sich auf die Lauer, schoß hervor
Jagte die silberne Kugel. Am siebenten Tag
Sprang sie auf seinen Schoß, ließ sich streicheln und schnurrte.
Da kam er sich vor wie einer, der große Macht hat.
Er wiegte sie, bürstete sie, band ihr ein Band um den Hals.
Doch in der Nacht entsprang sie, drei Stockwerke tief
Und lief, nicht weit, nur dorthin, wo er sie
Gefunden hatte. Wo die Weidenschatten
Im Mondlicht wehten. An der alten Stelle
Flog sie von Stein zu Stein im rauhen Felle
Und schrie.

NUR DIE AUGEN

Tauft mich wieder
Womit?
Mit dem nächstbesten Wasser
Dem immer heiligen.
Legt mir die Hand auf
Gebt mir den nächstbesten Namen
Einen geschlechtslosen
Frühwind- und Tannennamen
Für das letzte Stück Wegs.
Verwandelt mich immerhin
Nur meine Augen laßt mir
Diese von jeher offen
Von jeher tauglich.

Swung back and forth, so the iron rings rattled.
She ate up all the flowers he brought home.
She knocked vases off the table, tore up the petals.
She didn't sleep at night, sat at the foot of his bed
Looking up at him with burning eyes.
After a week the curtains were torn to shreds,
His kitchen was strewn with garbage. He did nothing anymore,
Didn't read, didn't play the piano,
The nerve of his left eye twitched constantly.
He had made her a ball out of silver paper,
Which she had scorned for a long time. On the seventh day
She lay in wait, shot out,
Chased the silver ball. On the seventh day
She leapt up onto his lap, let herself by petted, and purred.
Then he felt like a person with great power.
He rocked her, brushed her, tied a ribbon around her neck.
But in the night she escaped, three floors down,
And ran, not far, just to the place where he
Had found her. Where the willows' shadows
Moved in the moonlight. Back in the same place
She flew from rock to rock in her rough coat
And screamed.

—S.L. Cocalis

ONLY THE EYES

Baptize me again
With what?
With the next best water
Ever holy.
Put your hand on me
Give me the next best name
One that is neuter
Like names of the early wind and fir trees
For the rest of the way.
Change me in spite of it all
Just leave me my eyes
These eyes that have always been open
Always useful.

—S.L. Cocalis

FRAUENFUNK

Eines Tages sprech ich im Rundfunk
Gegen Morgen wenn niemand mehr zuhört
Meine gewissen Rezepte

Gießt Milch ins Telefon
Laßt Katzen hecken
In der Geschirrspülmaschine
Zerstampft die Uhren im Waschtrog
Tretet aus Euren Schuhen

Würzt den Pfirsich mit Paprika
Und das Beinfleisch mit Honig

Lehrt eure Kinder das Füchsinneneinmaleins
Dreht die Blätter im Garten auf ihre Silberseite
Beredet euch mit dem Kauz

Wenn es Sommer wird zieht euren Pelz an
Trefft die aus den Bergen kommen
Die Dudelsackpfeifer
Tretet aus Euren Schuhen

Seid nicht so sicher
Daß es Abend wird
Nicht so sicher
Daß Gott euch liebt.

WOMEN'S BROADCAST

Someday I'll announce on the radio
Towards morning when no one is listening
Certain recipes of mine

Pour milk into the telephone
Let cats breed
In the dishwasher
Stamp on watches in the wash basin
Kick off your shoes

Season a peach with paprika
And spread honey on meat

Teach your children the basic skills of female foxes
Turn the leaves in the garden over on the silver side
Discuss something with an odd-ball

When it is summer, put on your furs
Meet the men coming down from the mountains
The bagpipe players
Kick off your shoes

Don't be so sure
That evening will fall
Not so sure
That God loves you.

—S.L. Cocalis

INTERVIEW MIT MIR SELBST

Ich bin vor nicht zu langer Zeit geboren
In einer kleinen, klatschbeflissenen Stadt,
Die eine Kirche, zwei bis drei Doktoren
Und eine große Irrenanstalt hat.

Mein meistgesprochenes Wort als Kind war «nein».
Ich war kein einwandfreies Mutterglück.
Und denke ich an jene Zeit zurück:
Ich möchte nicht mein Kind gewesen sein.

Im letzten Weltkrieg kam ich in die achte
Gemeindeschule zu Herrn Rektor May.
—Ich war schon zwölf, als ich noch immer dachte,
Daß, wenn die Kriege aus sind, Frieden sei.

Zwei Oberlehrer fanden mich begabt,
Weshalb sie mich—zwecks Bildung—bald entfernten;
Doch was wir auf der hohen Schule lernten,
Ein Wort wie «Abbau» haben wir nicht gehabt.

Beim Abgang sprach der Lehrer von den Nöten
Der Jugend und vom ethischen Niveau—
Es hieß wir sollten jetzt ins Leben treten.
Ich aber leider trat nur ins Büro.

Acht Stunden bin ich dienstlich angestellt
Und tue eine schlechtbezahlte Pflicht.
Am Abend schreib ich manchmal ein Gedicht.
(Mein Vater meint, das habe noch gefehlt.)

Bei schönem Wetter reise ich ein Stück
Per Bleistift auf der bunten Länderkarte.
—An stillen Regentagen aber warte
Ich manchmal auf das sogenannte Glück...

MASCHA KALÉKO (1912–1975)

INTERVIEW WITH MYSELF

I was born not too long ago
In a small, gossip-loving town
With one church, doctors—three or so—
And one large mental institution.

As a child my favorite word was "no."
No perfect mama's girl was I.
And if I think of times gone by—
I'm glad I'm not my child, I know.

In the First World War, I was assigned
To a district school led by Rector May.
I was twelve already, still inclined
To think that peace would follow war one day.

Two high school teachers thought me intelligent
And sent me off to be educated.
Yet whatever learning we accumulated,
We didn't learn words like "retrenchment."

At graduation a teacher spoke about
The lofty goals, the needs of youth.
They said we must enter life, set out,
I entered an office in all truth.

For eight hours I am employed in service
And perform the tasks I'm underpaid to do.
On some evenings I'll write poetry too.
(My father says: "I really needed this!")

When the weather's nice, I travel, yes,
By pencil on a brightly colored map.
—On rainy days, hands in my lap,
I sometimes wait for so-called happiness...

—S.L. Cocalis

GROßSTADTLIEBE

Man lernt sich irgendwo ganz flüchtig kennen
Und gibt sich irgendwann ein Rendezvous.
Ein Irgendwas,—'s ist nicht genau zu nennen—
Verführt dazu, sich gar nicht mehr zu trennen.
Beim zweiten Himbeereis sagt man sich «du».

Man hat sich lieb und ahnt im Grau der Tage
Das Leuchten froher Abendstunden schon.
Man teilt die Alltagssorgen und die Plage,
Man teilt die Freuden der Gehaltszulage,
...Das übrige besorgt das Telephon.

Man trifft sich im Gewühl der Großstadtstraßen.
Zu Hause geht es nicht. Man wohnt möbliert.
—Durch das Gewirr von Lärm und Autorasen,
—Vorbei am Klatsch der Tanten und der Basen
Geht man zu zweien still und unberührt.

Man küßt sich dann und wann auf stillen Bänken,
—Beziehungsweise auf dem Paddelboot.
Erotik muß auf Sonntag sich beschränken.
...Wer denkt daran, an später noch zu denken?
Man spricht konkret und wird nur selten rot.

Man schenkt sich keine Rosen und Narzissen,
Und schickt auch keinen Pagen sich ins Haus.
—Hat man genug von Weekendfahrt und Küssen,
Läßt mans einander durch die Reichspost wissen
Per Stenographenschrift ein Wörtchen: «aus»!

LOVE IN THE CITY

Somewhere you meet each other—fleeting—
And sometimes there's a rendezvous.
A something, —it's not worth repeating—
Tempts you to prolong the meeting.
With the second sundae you say "du."

You like each other and anticipate by day
The promise of a night not spent alone.
You'll share the daily worries and dismays,
You'll share the joys of a raise in pay,
...The rest is done by telephone.

In the city's tumult you both meet.
Not at home. You live in a room in an apartment.
—Through the confusion, noise, cars on the street,
—Past the gossiping women and girls on their beat,
You go with each other, quiet, confident.

You kiss on a bench along the way,
—Or on a paddle-boat instead.
Eros must be limited to Sundays.
—You think of now—and come what may!
You speak bluntly and do not turn red.

You don't give each other narcissi or roses,
And you don't communicate by servant:
—When weekend kisses cease to engross,
Then you send a letter via Federal Post:
"It's over!" written down in shorthand.

—*S.L. Cocalis*

MANNEQUINS

Inserat: «*Mannequin 42er Figur,*
leichte, angenehme Arbeit, gesucht...»

Nur lächeln und schmeicheln den endlosen Tag...
Das macht schon müde.
—Was man uns immer versprechen mag:
Wir bleiben solide.
Wir prunken in Seide vom «dernier cri»
Und wissen: gehören wird sie uns nie.
Das bleibt uns verschlossen.
Wir tragen die Fähnchen der «Inventur»
Und sagen zu Dämchen mit Speckfigur:
«Gnäfrau,...wie angegossen!»

Wir leben am Tage von Stullen und Tee.
Denn das ist billig.
Manch einer spendiert uns ein feines Souper,
...Ist man nur willig.
Was nützt schon der Fummel aus Crêpe Satin—
Du bleibst, was du bist: Nur ein Mannequin.
Da gibts nichts zu lachen.
Wir rechnen, obs Geld noch bis Ultimo langt,
Und müssen trotzdem, weils die Kundschaft verlangt,
Das sorglose Püppchen machen.

Die Beine, die sind uns Betriebskapital
Und Referenzen.
Gehalt: so *hoch* wie die Hüfte *schmal.*
Logische Konsequenzen...
Bedingung: stets vollschlank, diskret und—lieb.
(Denn das ist der Firma Geschäftsprinzip.)
Und wird mal ein Wort nicht gewogen,
Dann sei nicht gleich prüde und schrei nicht gleich «Nee!»
Das gehört doch nun mal zum Geschäftsrenommée
Und ist im Gehalt einbezogen.

MANNEQUINS

Wanted: Model, with a size 6 figure.
Easy, pleasant work...

Just smiling and flattering the whole day through...
It gets you down.
—Whatever they promise to do:
We remain sound.
We show off in silks the *dernier cri*,
Knowing: they will never belong to me.
That door is closed to us.
We wear the rags from the stockroom,
And say to the damsels with figures "in bloom":
"Madam,...it's marvelous!"

We live from day to day on bread, butter, and tea.
We have to make do.
And sometimes a gentleman takes us to eat...
...If we want to.
What good is this wrapping of crèpe satin—
You are what you are: just a mannequin.
That's nothing to laugh at.
We worry about every cent at night,
Yet we must, like toy dolls, appear bright
Lest the customers complain about that.

Our legs are our working capital,
And our references.
Salary: as high as our hips are small.
Logical consequences...
Condition: well-proportioned, discreet, and—lovely,
(For that's the store's policy.)
And if men have something off-color to say,
Don't cry "No!" and don't show your shame.
It's all part of the company's name
And part of your pay.

—S.L. Cocalis

WAHRLICH

Für Anna Achmatova

Wem es ein Wort nie verschlagen hat,
und ich sage es euch,
wer bloß sich zu helfen weiß
und mit den Worten—

dem ist nicht zu helfen.
Über den kurzen Weg nicht
und nicht über den langen.

Einen einzigen Satz haltbar zu machen,
auszuhalten in dem Bimbam von Worten.

Es schreibt diesen Satz keiner,
der nicht unterschreibt.

ALLE TAGE

Der Krieg wird nicht mehr erklärt,
sondern fortgesetzt. Das Unerhörte
ist alltäglich geworden. Der Held
bleibt den Kämpfen fern. Der Schwache
ist in die Feuerzonen gerückt.
Die Uniform des Tages ist die Geduld,
die Auszeichnung der armselige Stern
der Hoffnung über dem Herzen.

Er wird verliehen,
wenn nichts mehr geschieht,
wenn das Trommelfeuer verstummt,
wenn der Feind unsichtbar geworden ist
und der Schatten ewiger Rüstung
den Himmel bedeckt.

Er wird verliehen
für die Flucht von den Fahnen,

INGEBORG BACHMANN (1926–1973)

TRULY

For Anna Ackmatova

Whoever has not choked on a word,
and I'm telling you,
whoever knows how to help oneself
—especially with words—

cannot be helped.
Not in the short run
and not in the long run.

To make one single sentence lasting,
to survive in the ding-dong of words.

No one writes this sentence
who doesn't sign.

—S.L. Cocalis

EVERY DAY

War is no longer declared,
it is continued. The unprecedented
takes place every day. The hero
stays far from the lines. The weakling
has been moved to the front.
The uniform of the day is patience,
bedecked with the modest star
of hope upon the heart.

It is awarded
when nothing more happens,
when the artillery stops,
when the enemy is no longer to be seen
and the shadow of perpetual armament
covers the sky.

It is awarded
for deserting the flag,

für die Tapferkeit vor dem Freund,
für den Verrat unwürdiger Geheimnisse
und die Nichtachtung
jeglichen Befehls.

ICH BIN KEIN INSEKT

Ich bin kein Insekt
Aber insektenmäßig
Bin ich auf den Rücken gefallen
Meine Beine
Suchen den Boden in der Luft
Ich habe Glück
Ich kippe mich seitlich um
Ich befinde mich auf meinen Füßen
Ich mache Gehversuche
Es geht Ich gehe
Aber jemand erinnert sich an sein Spiel
Jemandem nutzen meine Gehversuche überhaupt nichts
Jemand dessen Spiel ich verdarb
Legt mich ganz freundlich zurück
Das Spiel hat experimentellen Charakter
Ich bin wieder auf dem Rücken
So bin ich brauchbar
In Rückenlage bin ich einige Beobachtungen wert
Sofern ich mich in mein Pech schicke
Ich bin Lehrstoff
Ich diene dem Fortschritt
Mit mir kann man etwas beweisen.

for courage in facing the friend,
for betraying loathsome secrets
and for disobeying
every command.

—*Kate Flores*

GABRIELE WOHMANN (1932–)

I AM NOT A BUG

I am not a bug
But like a bug
I have fallen on my back
My legs
Search for the ground in the air
I am lucky
I tip over on my side
And find myself on my feet
I attempt to walk
It works I walk
But someone is reminded of his game
To that someone my efforts to walk are of no use at all
Someone whose game I spoiled
Puts me back amicably
The game is of an experimental nature
I'm on my back again
This way I'm useful
On my back I'm worthy of observation
As long as I can accept my bad luck
I can be used in the classroom
I serve the cause of progress
One can demonstrate something with me.

—*S.L. Cocalis*

ÜBELTÄTER

Jemand is beunruhigt
(Meinetwegen)
Es wird gewartet
(Ich fehle)
Rufe, umsonst
(Mein Name)
Ein Herz leidet unter Sauerstoffmangel
(Mir recht)
Man hat sie in eine Anstalt gebracht
(Ich wars, ich habe nichts dagegen)
Streit, Traurigkeit
(Meine Schuld)

Plötzlich, während der ersten Abenddämmerung, ein Opfer—
(Nicht von mir).

WIEDER IST ALLES GANZ GUT GEGANGEN

Wieder ist alles ganz gut gegangen
Ich habe die Post erledigt
Mir nichts einreden lassen
Myrna Wagner getroffen
Mich nicht entscheiden können
Zugegriffen
Schön gefunden
Etwas weniger schön gefunden
Auch die Nachmittagspost erledigt
Nochmal mich geweigert
Und bei meinem zweiten Gang zum Briefkasten
Ein zweites Mal Myrna Wagner gesehen
Nur von weitem
Also einen Umweg ums Viereck gemacht
Es fing an mir gegen den Strich zu gehen
Aber ich nahm mich zusammen
Fand die Town Hall-Streichhölzer
Konnte das Angebot annehmen
Hörte den Gärtner im Teichbecken herumknirschen

EVILDOER

Someone is upset
(On my account)
They are waiting
(I am missing)
Cries, in vain
(My name)
A heart suffers from lack of oxygen
(All right)
They have taken her to an institution
(It was I, I have nothing against it)
Quarrel, depression
(My fault)

Suddenly, during the first twilight, a sacrifice—
(Not mine).

—Margaret Woodruff

AGAIN EVERYTHING HAS GONE QUITE WELL

Again everything has gone quite well
I have finished with the mail
Not let myself be talked into anything
Met Myrna Wagner
Not been able to make up my mind
Fallen to
Liked it fine
Liked it somewhat less
Finished with the afternoon mail as well
Once more refused
And during my second walk to the mailbox
Seen Myrna Wagner a second time
Only from a distance
Therefore gone roundabout the square
It began to go against the grain for me
But I pulled myself together
Found the Town Hall matches
Was able to accept the offer
Heard the gardener crunch around in the bottom of the pond

Sah immer noch hin
Hielt es immer noch für bedeutungslos
Ich machte mir außerdem darüber Gedanken
Später später
Fügte mich
Gab unter gewissen Bedingungen nach
Die Getränke bei den Gaisbergs waren vorzüglich, auch die
    Häppchen
Also ging alles wiedermal ganz gut—
Aber vor dem Einschlafen habe ich doch erneut an das Gangrän
    gedacht
An das nicht einschläfernde Wort Tod
Kein Sedativum gewußt gegen Ewigen Schlaf
Und den blöden neuen Bezirk des Friedhofs vor mir gesehen
Den miesen Kiesweg im Nordteil
Wo sie die Toten dieses Jahres hinlegen
Und dann rechterhand neben dem Grab von Herbert Strecker
Und dem unbenutzten Platz zur Linken
Sein Grab
Zu dem mir nichts einfällt
Für das ich mich nicht erwärmen kann—
Bis es dann doch anfing
Mit Schlaf, Traum
Von nichts Besonderem
Worauf demnach festzustellen ist
Daß es wiedermal ganz gut ging.

Kept on watching
Kept on believing it to be meaningless
Moreover I thought about it
Later later
Acquiesced
Gave in under certain conditions
The drinks at the Gaisbergs' were excellent, also the snacks
So everything was going quite well once again—
But before going to sleep I thought again about gangrene
About the non-soporific word Death
Knew no sedative against Eternal Sleep
And saw the idiotic new section of the cemetery before me
The wretched gravel path in the north part
Where they lay the dead of this year
And then on the right-hand side next to the grave of Herbert Strecker
And the unused plot on the left
His grave
About which nothing occurs to me
Which does not inspire me—
Until it did begin
With sleep, dreams
About nothing in particular
Whereupon accordingly it can be established
That all went quite well again.

—*Margaret Woodruff*

BRIEF AN MEDEA

Medea du Schöne dreh dich nicht um
vierzig Talente hat er dafür erhalten
von der Stadt Korinth
der Lohnschreiber der
daß er dir den Kindermord unterjubelt
ich rede von Euripides verstehst du
seitdem jagen sie dich durch unsere Literaturen
als Mörderin Furie Ungeheuer
dabei hätte ich dich gut verstanden
wer nichts am Bein hat
kann besser laufen
aber ich sehe einfach nicht ein
daß eine schuldbeladene Gemeinde
ihre blutigen Hände an deinen Röcken abwischt
keine Angst wir machen
das noch publik
daß die Korinther selber deine zehn Gören gesteinigt haben
(wie sie schon immer mit Zahlen umgegangen sind)
und das mitten in Heras Tempel
Gewalt von oben hat keine Scham
na ja die Männer die Stadträte
machen hier so lustig weiter
wie früher und zu hellenischen Zeiten
(Sklaven haben wir übrigens auch)
bloß die Frauen kriegen neuerdings
Kinder auf Teufel komm raus
anstatt bei Verstand zu bleiben
(darin sind sie dir ähnlich)
andererseits haben wir
uns schon einigermaßen aufgerappelt
was ich dir noch erzählen wollte: die Callas ist tot

HELGA NOVAK (1935–)

LETTER TO MEDEA

Medea, you beautiful person, don't turn around
he received forty Talents for it
from the city of Corinth
the hack writer he
who pinned infanticide on you
I mean Euripides you know
since then they've chased you through literatures
as murderess fury and monster
and yet I would have understood you well
those who have nothing bound to their legs
can run better
but I just do not understand
how a guilt-ridden community
wipes off its bloody hands on your skirts
don't be afraid we'll make
it public yet
that the Corinthians themselves stoned your ten kids
(just like they always treat numbers)
and in the temple of Hera at that
official violence knows no shame
oh well the men of the town council
are carrying on jovially
just as before and in the Hellenic era
(we have slaves too by the way)
it's just that the women of late
are bearing children like mad
instead of keeping their wits about them
(in that they resemble you)
on the other hand we have
got back on our feet to a certain extent
another thing that I wanted to tell you: Callas is dead

—*S.L. Cocalis*

LAGEBERICHT

viele von uns sitzen noch
zornig
am Schreibtisch
viele von uns laufen noch
frei
herum
viele von uns schießen noch
gegen uns
mit ihren Gnadengesuchen
viele von uns denken noch
sie kämen durch
wenn sie ganz ruhig bleiben

FRÜHLING IM WESTEND

immergrüne Koniferen
überwuchern die frühern Jahreszeiten

geläufiger als die Vögel
sind uns die Namen ihrer Futtersorten

wo ist die Sonnenseite
auch die Rose ist keine Rose ist keine Rose mehr

in einigen Fällen
ist Dynamit der kürzeste Weg zum Licht

REPORT ON THE SITUATION

many of us are still sitting
angry
at our desks
many of us are still running
around
free
many of us are still shooting
against us
with their petitions for mercy
many of us still think
they will make it through
if they just keep real quiet

—*S.L. Cocalis*

SPRING IN WESTEND

evergreen conifers
overrun the earlier seasons

more familiar than the birds
are the names of different bird seeds

where is the sunny side
also the rose is no longer a rose is no longer a rose

in some cases
dynamite is the shortest way to the light

—*S.L. Cocalis*

MIR GEHT ES GUT

Mir geht es gut.
Er sagt Liebling zu mir
und sonntags essen wir Fleisch.
Ich lebe frei und friedlich
hier in der Bundesrepublik Deutschland
wo ich eingelocht werde
in eine Personalakte
wo ich eingestuft werde
in eine Lohngruppe
wo ich entlassen werde auf ein Girokonto.
Wo die Freizeit das Gaspedal durchdrückt
und ein Stückchen Natur mietet
einen Parkplatz für Zelte.
Ich bin zufrieden.
Er liebt seinen Garten
am Stadtrand.
Er gräbt.
Ich liebe Menschen.
Ich spiele Hände aus
ich reize zu hoch.
Ich buche einen Kuß
als Vorschuß ab.
Ich amüsiere mich
mit Stellung Nummer 12.
Mein Körper geht ohne Beanstandung
durch die Inspektion.
Liebe wird auf die hohe Kante gelegt
für schlechtere Zeiten.
Namen grüßen mich:
Ich grüße zurück.
Freunde laden mich ein:
Ich bin geladen.
Morgens, wenn Auspuffgase
die Hände der Bäume ergreifen
morgens, wenn ich verschlafen
Brote belege
weiß ich, mir geht es gut:
Meine Lebensversicherung wird
automatisch abgebucht.
Ich lebe ruhig zwischen Schreien:

MARGOT SCHROEDER (1937–)

I'M DOING FINE

I'm doing fine.
He says Honey to me
and there's meat on Sundays.
My life is free and peaceful
here in the Federal Republic of Germany
where I am punched into a computer card
for my dossier
where I am assigned
to an income group
where I am discharged to a bank account.
Where leisure time presses the gas pedal down
and a small piece of nature rents
a place to park tents.
I am satisfied.
He loves his garden plot
on the outskirts of town.
He digs.
I love people.
I play my hands out
my bids are too high.
I give him a kiss
as partial payment.
I amuse myself
with position number 12.
My body passes inspection
without any problem.
Love's put away
for hard times.
Names greet me:
I greet them back.
Friends ask me over:
I am charged to come.
In the morning, when muffler emissions
take the hands of the trees
in the morning, when sleepily I
make the sandwiches
then I know I'm doing fine:
my life insurance premiums are
automatically deducted.
I live quietly between screams:

Bremsschreien
Modeschreien
Eheschweigen.

Manchmal breche ich aus.
Die Kinder weinen mich zurück.
Also bleibe ich,
also verbrenne ich nervös
eine Zigarettenkette.
Wenn im Fernsehraster
napalmgebrannte Kinder
auf meine Salzstangengitter
zulaufen
und ich beiläufig sage:
Das Bild ist unscharf
weiß ich—
ich bin zuhause.

ICH DENKE AN DICH

Ich denke an dich.
Ich sehe dich
hinter deiner Brille wohnen.
Deine Schreie
treffen andere Schreie
im Adreßbuch deiner Stadt.
Du bist so frei
wie dein Schwur
frei zu sein.
Zwei Finger einer Hand
sind keine Faust.
Auch ich bin ein Krüppel
aus Zeigefingern
—vorläufig—
Aber dieses Wort,
sprich es langsam aus,
ist eine Revolution.

Ich liebe meinen Hängebusen.
Meine Schwangerschaftsnarben.

screaming brakes
screaming fashions
conjugal silence.

I escape sometimes.
The children cry me back.
Thus I remain,
thus I am nervous, I burn
a chain of cigarettes.
When on the TV screen
napalmburned children
run on
my pretzelstick-grid
and I say casually:
the picture's not clear
I know—
I am at home.

—S.L. Cocalis

I'M THINKING OF YOU

I'm thinking of you.
I see you
living behind your glasses.
Your cries
meet other cries
in the address book of your city.
You are as free
as your vow
to be free.
Two fingers of one hand
are not a fist.
I too am a cripple,
all index-fingers
—for now—
But this word,
speak it slowly,
is a revolution.

I love my sagging breasts.
My stretch marks.

Ich liebe die Apfelsinenhaut
auf meinen Oberschenkeln.
Im Urteil der Männer
verblüht.
Ich sage: Die Saat geht auf.
Ich bin schön
wenn ich lache
wenn meine Tränensäcke
Falten schlagen.
Ich bin kein Wesen
mit falschen Wimpernflügeln.

Ich, erntereif:
Ein trauriges Ereignis,
ein Mädchen nur.
Vater ließ seine Enttäuschung
als Kornflasche kreisen,
Mutter sperrte mich ein
in rosa Wäsche.
Sie nannten mich Baby.
Baby. Sagte mein erster Freund
und die Freunde danach:
Sugarbaby
Honeybaby
Superbaby.
Aus den Windeln kam ich nicht heraus.
Im Laufstall lernte ich
gerade zu stehen.
Ich lernte gehorchen.
Und horchen.
Abhorchen.
Ich fuhr meine Herzklappen aus
ich flog davon.
Keine Blinde mehr
auf den Seiten für Leserbriefe.
Ich lernte sehen.

Ich lernte zuhören.
Ich höre zu
dem Schnapsgewaltigen in der Kneipe,
wenn er die gleitende Arbeitszeit
verflucht
weil er jeden Klogang
in der Stechkarte wiederfindet.
Der Nachbarin
für die ein zähes Beefsteak
eine Naturkatastrophe ist.

I love the orangepeelskin
on my thighs.
In the opinion of men:
withered flower.
I say: I'm bearing fruit.
I am beautiful
when I laugh
when the bags hanging under my eyes
melt in wrinkles.
I'm not a creature
with false-eyelashwings.

I, ripe to be harvested:
a sad occurrence,
it's only a girl.
Father passed disappointment around
with his bottle;
Mother imprisoned me
in pink swathing.
They called me Baby.
Baby. My first boyfriend said it
and the other ones after him:
Sugarbaby
Honeybaby
Superbaby.
I never got out of my diapers.
In the playpen I learned
to stand up straight.
I learned to obey.
And to listen.
To eavesdrop.
I opened the valves of my heart
I ran away.
No longer blind
to the pages for letters to editors
I learned to see.

I learned to listen.
I listen to
the tough drunk in a bar
when he curses the sliding-time
workday
since now every trip to the john
is punched on his card.
To the neighbor
for whom a tough beefsteak
is a natural disaster.

Ich klage an
den freien
sozialen Markt
auf dem meine Haut
gehandelt wird
wie ein Schafsfell:
barbiert
strapazierfähig
trittfest.

SOZIALISMUS, SAG ICH

Der Dichter G. B. sagt über sich selbst:
Ihm fehle das Urvertrauen,
für seine Frau Mutter empfinde er Haß,
drum sei er Freudianer.
Seinen Sauberkeitszwang halte er
peinlich vor Putzfrauen geheim.
Positivist sei er einmal gewesen,
im Vordergrund stehe bei ihm schlicht der Schwanz.
Wenn du dir 's leisten kannst, sag ich.
Ob deine Identität nicht vielleicht verhindert wurde?
Wenn G. B. vom Trinken genug hat,
weint er und redet von Selbstmord.
Todestrieb, ja.
Widerstand leistet er nicht.
Er wird von zahlreichen Mädchen
als unglücklicher Dichter verwöhnt.
Sein Hirn hängt voller Girlanden
von all den poetischen Festen,
und seine Gedanken, die sitzen
erstklassig in fahrenden Zügen herum.
Da er sich noch an sich gewöhnen müsse,
sagt er, könne er sich nicht organisieren.
Ach, Kleingläubiger, glaub doch an Gott.

I accuse
the free
social market
in which my skin
is traded
like sheepskin:
barbered
durable
nice underfoot.

—*S.L. Cocalis*

UTE ERB (1940–)

SOCIALISM, I SAY

The poet G.B. says about himself:
He lacks that primal trust,
he feels hate for his mother
thus he's a Freudian.
Because he's embarrassed he hides his cleanliness fetish
from cleaning ladies.
He once was a logical positivist,
everything else must come after his prick.
If you can afford it, I say.
Hasn't your identity perhaps become impaired?
When G.B. has had too much to drink,
he cries and speaks of suicide.
Death-wish, yes.
He doesn't offer resistance.
He is spoiled by numerous girls
as the suffering poet.
His brain is hung with garlands
from all of the poetic parties,
and his ideas, they are sitting,
first class, in travelling trains.
As he still has to get used to himself,
he says, he can't get organized.
Oh, ye of no faith, just believe in the Lord!

Glaubenstrieb, Todestrieb,
Anhänger-zum-Triebwagen-Trieb.
Sozialismus, sag ich,
ist eine Sache für seßhafte Leute.
Ich sehe viel Wissenschaft vor mir,
mich seh ich als Putzfrau.
In meinem Gehirn die Gedanken
laufen treppab, treppauf und fegen und wischen.
Ich lebe davon,
andern Leuten den Dreck wegzumachen
aus ihren Gehirnen.

EIN UNGENÜGEN

Wenn ich allein bin, sagt mir keiner, wer ich bin.
Im Spiegel finde ich mich stumm,
die Zeit vergeht, ich bleibe sitzen.
Hinter meinen Ohren steckt
der Ekel vorm Gedränge.

Wenn ich mit vielen bin,
genügen sie mir nicht.
Ich renne, renne, renne
allen nach.

ABSTAMMUNG

woher soll ich wissen wer ich bin?
von kindheit um meine welt betrogen,
meine geschichte kaum überliefert.
ein nebensatz im geschichtsbuch:
...wurden im laufe der inquisition auch millionen frauen verbrannt.

Belief-wish, death-wish,
Railway-car-follower-wish.
Socialism, I say,
is a matter for the sedentary.
I see lots of knowledge before me,
myself I see as a cleaning lady.
And in my brain the ideas are
running downstairs, upstairs, are sweeping and polishing.
I'm making a living of
cleaning up the dirt from the brains
of others.

—*S.L. Cocalis*

A DEFICIENCY

When I am alone, no one tells me who I am.
In the mirror I find myself silent,
time passes, I sit there.
Behind my ears lurks
my loathing of crowds.

When I'm with a lot of people,
they aren't enough for me.
I chase, chase, chase
after everyone.

—*S.L. Cocalis*

BARBARA FIEDLER (1942–)

ORIGINS

whence should i know who i am?
cheated of my world from childhood on,
my history hardly handed down.
a dependent clause in the history book:
   . . .during the inquisition millions of women were also burned to
      death.

eine widmung: meiner lieben lebensgefährtin, ohne deren
aufopferung, hilfe, verständnis dies werk
nicht entstanden wäre.
ein privatbrief: die wärme meiner hündlein des nachts ist so tröstlich,
schreibt lieselotte vom französischen hof.

woher soll ich wissen, wie ich bin?
ich habe die maske nicht geschnitzt bemalt aufgesetzt.
vorgepreßte schönheit liegt fordernd über meiner haut,
die form meiner jochbögen ist nicht perfekt,
meine augenbrauen ziehen fremde furchen in unvollkommener
    gegend
tastend fühle ich den schwung meiner lippen nach: es reicht nicht.

woher soll ich wissen, was ich bin?
nichts um mich aus mir.
ich habe mich nie beschrieben; das mythenkorsett
ist aufgezwungen: große mutter, schädelklirrende kali
oder liebende göttin—vorgegebne bilder,
männer haben sie ausgemalt, mir
blitzschnell die lider zugenäht.
warum darf ich meinen augen
nicht trauen?

woher soll ich die farbe meiner träume kennen?
nachtschwarz oder morgenrot ist im dunklen
nicht zu unterscheiden. ich riß mir die brust auf,
adams rippe zurückzugeben, habe
dann leichter atmend eine haarsträhne
in warme wundflüssigkeit getaucht,
male nun mit sperrigem pinsel. allmählich
fängt höhlenwand licht, ich beginne
zu unterscheiden, bald
werde ich sehen, und morgen
werde ich wissen, wer ich bin.

a dedication: for my dear partner in life, without whose
devotion, help, understanding this work
could not have been written.
a private letter: the warmth of my little puppy at night is so
    comforting,
writes liselotte of the french court.

whence should i know how i am?
i put on the mask i didn't carve or paint.
preformed beauty lies demandingly on my skin,
the form of my yoke-arches isn't perfect,
my eyebrows are plowing strange furrows in imperfect land.
groping, i feel for the curve of my lips:
it isn't enough.

whence should i know what i am?
nothing around me of me.
i never described myself; the corset of myths
is forced upon me: great mother, skullrattling kali,
or loving goddess—inherited images,
painted by men, my
eyes are sewn shut in an instant.
why may i not trust
my eyes?

whence should i know the color of my dreams?
midnight black or dawn red look the same
in the dark, i rip open my breast
to give back adam's rib, then
breathing easier, i dip a lock of hair
into the wound's warm liquid.
i paint with a cumbersome brush. gradually,
the cave walls catch fire, i'm starting
to learn the difference, soon
i will see, and tomorrow
i'll know who i am.

—S.L. Cocalis

AUFKLÄRUNGSSTUNDE

Manchmal im Lauf der Geschichte
hat man uns
den kleinen Finger gereicht
und als wir dann
die ganze Hand nehmen wollten
ist es bei Licht und Verstand besehen
doch nur ein Pimmel gewesen

Ach du heiliger Bimbam
das war wohl der falsche Griff
da sind wir doch jedesmal unfreiwillig
an die falsche Spezies geraten
an eine abgelebte Art
die pars pro toto immer noch weiterspukt
an den Appendixband einer überkommenen Philosophie

Ungläubig staunend und voll enzyklopädischer Neugier
betrachten wir jetzt die letzten Exemplare
dieser omnipotenten Eroberer
mit gratis verliehenem Orden unter dem Feigenblatt
dieser lärmenden Greifschwanzäffchen
mit funktionslos leierndem Imponiergehabe

Dieses weltbewegende Zipfelchen
erkennen wir nun
das war immer nur
das dicke Ende einer Schnur
an der man Hampelmänner springen läßt

Und wie sie sich abgestrampelt haben
die Hacken haben sie sich abgerannt
in die Knie sind sie gegangen
und wieder aufgestanden
ihre Ellenbogen haben sie benutzt
die Hände aufgehalten
und ab und zu
ihre Finger krummgemacht

Einiges allerdings hat sich
hinter ihrem Rücken abgespielt und
so ein Marionettentheater
ist inzwischen nicht mehr gefragt

KARIN KIWUS (1942–)

LESSON ON THE FACTS OF LIFE

At times in the course of history
people have extended
a pinky to us
and then as we
wanted to take the whole hand
it turned out to be in the light of reason
only a little prick

Jeepers creepers
that was really a clinker
we always hit upon the
wrong species involuntarily
upon an extinct race
that continues to haunt us as *pars pro toto*
upon the appendix-volume of a handed-down philosophy

Incredulous amazed and full of encyclopedic curiosity
we now observe the last examples
of this omnipotent conqueror
with the distinction under the fig leaf that came gratis
this noisy ape with its prehensile tail
with nonfunctional ondroning selfaggrandizement

This little pecker that makes the whole world go round
we now understand it
it was always just
the thick end of a string
on which one lets jumping jacks dance

And when they were all danced out
they ran their feet off
and they went down on their knees
and got up again
they used their elbows
held up their hands
and now and then
bent their fingers

Some things however did occur
behind their backs and
such puppet shows
are no longer popular

weil wir heute alle ja
schon in die Schule gehn

wo wir zum Abschluß der Lektion
alles nochmal überprüfen wollen
sämtliche Jahrgänge der HUMAN REVIEW herbeiholen
und in jeder Nummer lesen können
schwarz auf weiß in der headline:

Der Pithecanthropus erectus
ist seit längerer Zeit
ausgestorben

HOMMES À FEMME

Wenn eine kleine unscheinbare Frau
lange kluge und ein wenig
lispelnde Reden hält
über Don Juan und Casanova
dann stehen so Männer auf
und zischen Herrgottnochmal
was soll das überhaupt
die ist doch viel zu fipsig dafür

because today we all
go to school

where at the end of the lesson
we want to check over everything
consult the collected volumes of the *Human Review*
and in each issue we can read
in black and white the headline:

For some time now
the Pithecanthropus erectus
has been extinct

—S.L. *Cocalis*

HOMMES A FEMME

If a small, homely woman
delivers long, intelligent and
slightly whispered speeches
on Don Juan and Casanova
then men will get up
and hiss goodgodinheaven
why does she bother
she isn't built for the job

—S.L. *Cocalis*

MAKE-OFF

Aus einer anderen Welt erscheine ich mir
    flackernd in diesem Spiegel
        als gefallener Engel
    ein Altarbild
                    unsrer lieben Frau
        von der gesellschaftsfähigen Schönheit
verhangen in den Tagesschatten
    abgeblitzt in einzelnen Momenten und tief
eingependelt zwischen verzerrten Mundwinkeln

Alle Poren spüre ich öffnen sich
    zu Löchern in der Luft
aus den Augen rinnt flüssiges Porzellan
    das Fliegennetz über den Haaren reißt
und dünn in Zweierreihen laufen
    die Ameisen aus unter den Nasenflügeln

Mein entführtes Gesicht ertaste ich
    sacht mit den Fingerspitzen
        ein paar Handgriffe noch wie im Schlaf
Reinigungsmilch unter die Haut Lotion auf die Tupfer
    erfrischen und glätten und alles regenerieren
und die Fassung zurückgewinnen en face und
    ein Aufwind im Dunstkreis über dem Körper
        eine Dusche und eine Emulsion
und drei vier Tropfen DNS endlich
    als Stärkung für den nächsten Tag

Die Adstringenzien regelmäßig
    nicht zu vergessen
        eine hingebungsvolle Pflege
und über Nacht
            über Nacht wenigstens im Traum
    paßt mein Bild wieder in seinen Rahmen

MAKE-OFF

From another world I appear to myself
   flickering in this mirror
      as a fallen angel
   an altar-painting
                     of our dear lady
      of socially viable beauty
veiled in the shadows of day
   rebuffed at some moments and deeply
swinging between the distorted poles of her smile

All my pores widening I can feel
   them holes in the air
from my eyes liquid porcelain's running
   the fly-netting over my hair tears
and thin in rows of two the ants march
   out from under the wings of my nose

I am exploring my abducted face
   lightly with my fingertips
      another few touches as reflex-actions
white facial cleanser under the skin lotion on the cotton pad
   to refresh and to smooth and to regenerate
and to regain composure *en face* and
   a current of air in the atmosphere up over my body
      a shower and an emulsion
and three four drops of DNA finally
   to fortify me for the next day

The regular use of an astringent tonic
   must not be omitted
      devoted care
and overnight
                  overnight at least in dreams
   my picture fits into its frame once again

—S.L. Cocalis

EIN ZEUGE

Ich sehe
den Staub
im Zimmer
nicht mehr
seit ich micn
zu mir
aufgemacht habe.

DIE KINDER DIE SIE

Die Kinder die sie
in viereckigen Sandkästen
großziehen
werden stelle ich mir vor
quadratisch sein
eingepaßt in die fruchtlosen
Vielecke der Vorstädte
begraben in immer den gleichen
Neubauwohnungen
eingespannt an Arbeitsplätzen
deren Nutzen ihnen eingeredet
aber nicht faßbar gemacht wird
registriert auf dem Rechteck
einer Karteikarte
auf Mikrofilm gespeichert
jährlich mit zwanzig Tonnen Blei
aus der Atemluft vollgepumpt
die Raupenpest in den Alleebäumen
wird von der Tagespresse
nicht mehr erwähnt
die Raupen

HELGA OSSWALD (1942–)

A WITNESS

I don't see
the dust
in my room
anymore
since I have
gone off
to myself.

—*S.L. Cocalis*

ANGELIKA MECHTEL (1943–)

THE CHILDREN THEY

The children they
rear
in fourcornered sandboxes
will I imagine
be rectangular
fitting into the barren
multicornered suburbs
buried in always the same
new high-rise apartments
harnessed to workplaces
whose advantages have been
drilled into them but not explained
registered in the upper right-hand corner
of a file card
stored on microfilm
annually pumped full with twenty tons
of lead from the atmosphere
the moth-infestation of the tree-lined streets
is no longer mentioned
by the papers
the caterpillars

könnten stelle ich mir vor
quadratisch sein
und einer hat die Idee
Sandkästen nicht mehr herzustellen

DEN REIS KOCHEN

Den Reis kochen
und das Fleisch
schneiden
ich tue es gern
für mich
der Gedanke dann
näher am Anfang
zu sein
du
könntest es heute
genauso
warum
tust du es nicht
für mich
Reis kochen
und das Fleisch
schneiden

could I imagine
be rectangular
and someone has an idea
to stop manufacturing sandboxes

—*S.L. Cocalis*

COOKING THE RICE

Cooking the rice
and cutting the
meat
I like to do it
for me
then the thought
to be
closer to the beginning
you
could do it today
just as well
why
don't you do it
for me
cook the rice
and cut the
meat

—*S.L. Cocalis*

STREICHELEINHEITEN

das ist gewiß ein sensibler mann
der beim spaziergang mit seiner frau
eine katze streichelt
stundenlang zärtlich streichelt

so daß die frau schon langsam weitergeht
stundenlang langsam weitergeht

MEINE VORLETZTE REDE AUF EINER ZUSAMMENKUNFT
EINIGER DIE GUTEN WILLENS SIND
KURZ VOR DER ABREISE DER MEISTEN

ich wünsche mir einen ruhigen platz
an dem ich überleben könnte
                          ohne alles aufzugeben
zum birnenschälen in ruhe
und kompottkochen für andere
zum gemeinsamen lesen und diskutieren
aufstehen könnten wir dort ungefragt
und ruhig und betont miteinander sprechen
auch fehler bemerken
                          ohne zeitliche beschränkung.
die blumen ums haus gediehen
                          ohne unser zutun
und die arbeit fürs gemüse könnten wir abends leisten.
die zeit bliebe nachzudenken
was wir tun sollten.

doch
meinen zorn über draußen
                          könnte ich erst vergeßen
wenn die berge versetzt sind.

FREDERIKE FREI (1945–)

STROKE UNITS

that is certainly a sensitive man,
who, while walking with his wife,
strokes a cat
for hours tenderly

so that the woman slowly goes her own way,
for hours slowly goes her own way.

—S.L. *Cocalis*

J. MONIKA WALTHER (1945–)

MY PENULTIMATE SPEECH AT A MEETING OF SOME PEOPLE OF GOOD WILL SHORTLY BEFORE MOST OF THEM LEAVE

i would like to have a quiet place
where i could survive
                        without giving up everything
a place for peeling pears in peace
and making preserves for the others
for communal reading and discussing
we could get up there as we pleased
and speak to each other quietly but firmly
and point out mistakes too
                        without temporal restrictions.
the flowers thrive around the house
                              without our assistance
and we can work evenings in the vegetable patch.
there would be time to think about
what we should do.

yet
i could only forget
            my rage about out there
if the mountains were moved.

die ereignisse und der ruhige platz dringen mir
als niederlage in mein herz
werft das verschimmelte auf den mist
beeilt euch beim birnenschälen
aber bleibt bedächtig.
laßt uns essen
gemeinsam und mit freude
in den spiegeln unsere gesichter ansehen
und mit dem zorn nach draußen gehen
und die herren der lage verstören
wir frauen werden im dunkeln vorauseilen
                              dies haben wir schon gelernt
für die kinder damals
aufwiedersehen schmerz.

aber was werden sie entscheiden
wo wir hingehen dürfen
wieviel werden sie uns geben
                              an raum und zeit
wie uns einsperren
welche letzte ruhestätten uns zuweisen
doch
wir haben gefühlt
                      und dies ist eine verteidigung
und wir wissen auch
genau und bewiesen
erfahren erlitten von anderen
schon zu oft
wie die verhältnisse sind:
wir werden nicht wollen
was sie uns zuordnen
was sie uns abgeben
wir wollen nicht stehenbleiben
auf dem zugewiesenen platz
und dort menschen sortieren
einordnen und in akten abheften
und die gewehre polieren
für die herren der lage.

the events and the peaceful place pierce my heart
as defeats
throw out the moldy stuff onto the compost heap
hurry up peeling the pears
but remain prudent
let us eat
communally and with joy
and look at ourselves in the mirror
and then go out there with our rage
and cause trouble for those men in charge
we women will run on ahead in the dark

                              we have learned this already

for the children then
farewell pain.

but what will they decide
where will we be able to go
how much time how much space

                    will they give us

how imprison us
show us our last resting place.
yet
we have felt
            and this is a defense
and we know too
exactly and proven
experienced suffered by others
too often already
what the scene is:
we will not want
what they decree for us
what they concede us
we don't want to stay
in the places they give us
to sort out people there
rank them and put them in files
and polish the weapons
for those men in charge.

—S.L. Cocalis

DIE FRAU, DIE SICH IM KOITUS MIT BEWEGT

Die frau, die sich im koitus mit bewegt
kommt von weit her
schaut sie genau an
die frau, auf der ihr liegt!
hinter ihr tun sich wüsten und abgründe auf.
sie hat lange strecken von vergessen zurück
gelegt, herzbrocken im geröll verstreut, felsen
vor frische wunden geschoben
ihre gefühle sind abgemagert.
jahre auf der eisdecke eurer ängste zugebracht
die zacken der gefühlsarmut gerundet so sanft
so samten so weich.
sie trägt ein meer
von angestauten orgasmen in sich, das sie
zu keinen lebzeiten wird ausgiessen können
die zeit drängt, die gedanken brennen, sie ist
eine ruferin in der wüste, die frau
auf der ihr liegt
schaut sie genau an!
nicht dieser warme körper
unter euch
ist wirklichkeit
was ihr für wirklich haltet, ist nur ein augen
blick, ein innehalten zwischen
vielen wirklichkeiten
davor und
danach

VERENA STEFAN (1947–)

THE WOMAN MOVING WITH YOU IN COITUS

The woman moving with you in coitus
comes from far away
look at her closely
the woman you lie upon!
behind her gape deserts and abysses.
she has put long stretches of forgetting
behind her, fragments of heart strewn in rubble,
boulders pushed before fresh wounds
her feelings are worn to the bone.
years spent on the icy sheet of your fears
the peaks of emotional poverty rounded so gently
so velvety so pliant.
she bears an ocean
of pent-up orgasms inside, which she
will never in a lifetime be able to pour out
time is of the essence, thoughts burn, she is
a cry in the wilderness, the woman
you lie upon
look at her closely!
not this warm body
beneath you
is reality
what you take for reality is only the bat
of an eye, a pause between
many realities before and
after

—*Johanna Moore and Beth Weckmueller*

HYMNE AUF DIE FRAUEN DER BÜRGERLICHEN KLASSE

Oh, diese gebändigte Schönheit der Frauen
der bürgerlichen Klasse. Der unnachahmliche
Fall ihrer Kleider. Ihre gezügelte Art
einen Fuß vor den anderen zu setzen und nie
       einen Schritt zurück.

Oh, diese schwingenden Lockenwellen
um ihre Schläfen und Ohren, diese fast
zufällig wirkende Ordnung in ihren Häusern
diese ausgewogenen Sätze, die sie sagen
       wenn man sie fragt.

Oh, ihr wissendes Lächeln über die Dummheiten
der Kinder, ihr höflicher, aber bestimmter
Ton für die Putzfrau, ihre kleine Freude
ein Seidentuch billig zu kaufen, das auch
       teuer bezahlt zählt.

Oh, ihr leuchtendes Nagelrot, die stillen Monde
der Fingernägel, auf denen nichts brennt
ihr dezentes Lippenrot, ihr beständiges
Fußnagelrot, das schon früh am Morgen
       für den Abend leuchtet.

Oh, ihre schmackhaften, bekömmlichen Mahlzeiten
serviert auf geschmackvollen Tellern
ihre Tischdecken, Kronleuchter, Kerzenständer
das Silber, die geschliffenen Gläser, rustikales
       Salatbesteck nicht zu vergessen.

Oh, dieser brennende Wunsch, dazuzugehören
die sanft gebogene Nase immer in die richtige
Sache zu stecken, die feinen Taschentücher
die Düfte, sorgsam ausgewählt zur jeweiligen
       Lage und Laune.

Oh, ihre Apfelsinenbäumchen und Azaleen
ihre Baumwollhemdchen, Seidenblusen
Kaschmirpullis, Skianzüge, Lederjäckchen
ihre Finkenpaare und Angorakater und
       das Pudelgrab im Garten.

Oh, und ihre verschwiegene Lust zwischen den Beinen
ihr schönes Keuchen, Hecheln, Schwitzen, die ganze

URSULA KRECHEL (1947–)

HYMN TO THE WOMEN OF THE MIDDLE CLASS

Oh, this subdued, subtle beauty of middle-class
women. The inimitable clothes that they wear.
Their restraint, placing one foot
in front of the other without ever
   a step backward.

Oh, these whirling, curled waves
on their temples and ears, oh, this order
that almost looks casual in all their houses,
these well-tempered sentences they say
   if one asks them.

Oh, their knowing smiles about their children's
nonsense, their polite but quite definite
tone with the servants, their joy at
buying a silk scarf cheaply that looks as if
   it had cost a lot.

Oh, their glowing nail polish, the quiet moons
of their fingernails, which are not burning,
their decent red lipstick, their perpetual
toenail polish that glows in the morning already
   for the evening to come.

Oh, their tasty, digestible repasts,
served on elegant china, their tablecloths,
chandeliers, candelabra, the silver,
the hand-cut crystal, not to mention the rustic
   salad service.

Oh, this burning desire, they want to belong,
to insert their gently arched noses in the right
places, the fine handkerchiefs, the fragrances,
carefully chosen for each situation
   and mood.

Oh, their miniature orange trees and their azaleas,
their cotton camisoles, blouses of silk, cashmere
pullovers, skiing outfits and leather jackets,
their matching canaries and angora cats and the
   poodle's grave in the garden.

Oh, and their discreet lust between legs,
their lovely gasping, panting, sweating, the

sorgfältig gepflegte Hingabe und alle Versuche
sich noch einmal vorteilhaft zu verändern
         beim Friseur.

Oh, ihre Anwandlungen von Schwermut, Heiterkeit
ihre einsamen Gedanken, wenn der Mann
noch in Geschäften unterwegs ist oder wo immer
ihr Aufschrecken beim kleinsten Geräusch
         in der Stille der Nacht.

Oh, ihre liebenswürdigen kleinen Abende
bei Kerzenschein, ihr untrügliches Gefühl
wer zu ihnen paßt und wer nicht, die Fähigkeit
sich anzupassen, zuzuhören, mitzureden
         über alles, wovon man spricht.

Oh, ihre langsam versiegende Kraft, die Panik
vor dem leeren Haus, den erwachsenen Kindern
ihre berechtigten Zweifel an der Treue aller
ihr Kränkeln im verdunkelten Schlafzimmer
         am hellen Tage.

Oh, und immer wieder die Selbstverständlichkeit
mit der sie noch einmal aufstehen, zwischen allen
Stühlen sitzen, die Zähne zusammenbeißen, Hände
schütteln als sei alles wie immer
         früher und jetzt.

WARNUNG

Komm aus der Höhe herab
steig mal von deinem Roß

sieh einfach zu und staune

wie ich den Kopf hebe
die Schultern, die Arme
davonfliege in klarer Luft
ohne mich umzusehen nach dir.

whole carefully tended surrender and all the attempts
to change to one's advantage yet once again at
    the beauty salon.

Oh, their fits of depression and cheerfulness
their lonely thoughts when the husband
is still out on business or wherever
their being startled by any small sound
    in the still of the night.

Oh, their charming little evenings by
candlelight, their unerring sense of
who fits in and who doesn't, the talent
to adapt, to belong, to put in a word about
    any topic.

Oh, their power that's slowly abating, the panic
of an empty house, grown up children,
their justified doubting of everyone's loyalty
their ailing in darkened bedrooms
    in broad daylight.

Oh, and again and again, the way that it goes without
saying, with which they get up again, sitting between
all the chairs, gritting their teeth, shaking hands,
as if everything was as before
    for now and forever.

—S.L. Cocalis

WARNING

Come down from your heights
come down off your high horse

just look and be amazed

at how I raise my head
my shoulders, my arms
and fly away in the clear sky
without looking back at you.

—S.L. Cocalis

NACH MAINZ!

Angela Davis, die Jungfrau Maria und ich
liegen in klammen weißen Betten
in einem Krankenhaus, dritte Klasse.
Wir reden nicht viel. Im Nebenraum
plärren die Säuglinge, die man uns abgepreßt hat.
Jede von uns ist an einem Wochentag
von einem gewöhnlichen Kind entbunden worden.
Maria liegt sehr blond in ihren Kissen.
Angela schläft viel. Ich lese in Freuds Traumdeutung
und frage mich, warum ich trotzdem
von pelzigen Säuge- und Nagetieren träume.
Pünktlich klopft eine Schwesternschülerin
und bringt die Düsseldorfer Nachrichten. Ausgerechnet
Düsseldorf, denke ich noch. Hier haben sie uns niedergestreckt.
Dann fällt mir die Schlagzeile auf: Zweite deutsche Teilung.
Alle Sozialisten nach Süddeutschland verbannt.
Demarkationslinie ist der Main.
Wir springen aus den Betten. Nichts wie nach Mainz
den Rhein hinauf. Wir umarmen uns, lachen
rennen barfuß durch die Altstadt zum Rhein.
Die Kinder, ruft Maria an einer roten Ampel.
Wir kehren nicht um. Die Nachkommen gehen eigene Wege.
Schon stehen wir bis zu den Knien in der grauen Brühe
bespritzen Brust und Arme und kraulen los.
Obwohl wir gegen den Strom schwimmen, kommen wir
gut voran. Was für ein Glück, die Arme auszustrecken
zu prusten, gurgeln, spritzen, um sich zu schlagen.
Hinter Wesseling ist das Wasser ganz klar.
Möwen begleiten uns eine Weile.
Während wir uns auf den Rücken werfen, reden wir
darüber, was uns erwartet. Ich kneife Angela in den Arm.
Wir träumen nicht. Am Loreleifelsen treffen wir
tatsächlich einen Fischer in seinem Nachen.
Er rudert gemächlich, damit er sich unterhalten kann.
Später bittet er uns in seinen Kahn.
Besonders Maria weckt sein Interesse.
Sie gleiche einer bestimmten Person aufs Haar.
Manchmal schaut er ihr ins Gesicht. Bis nach Bingen
rudert er uns. Er zögert mitzukommen.
Einerseits sehe er unser historisches Glück
andererseits habe er Frau und Kinder.
Während wir ihm zuwinken, werden Boot und Mütze
kleiner und kleiner. Gegen Abend erreichen wir Mainz.

TO MAINZ!

Angela Davis, the Virgin Mary, and I
are lying in narrow white beds
in a hospital, third class.
We don't talk a lot. In the next room
the infants they have squeezed out of us are crying.
Each of us delivered a normal child
on a weekday.
Mary is very blonde on her pillows.
Angela sleeps a lot. I'm reading Freud's *Interpretation of Dreams*
and ask myself why I nevertheless
dream of furry mammals and rodents.
Punctually the student nurse knocks
and brings in the paper. Düsseldorf,
of all places, I'm thinking. Here's where they grounded us.
Then I see the headlines: Second Partition of Germany.
All Socialists Banished to Southern Germany.
Line of Demarcation the River Main.
We jump out of bed. We must get to Mainz,
down the Rhine. We all hug each other, laugh,
and run barefoot through the city, down toward the Rhine.
The children! Mary cries at a red light.
We don't turn around. Our offspring will go their own ways.
We are already knee-deep in the gray soup,
splash water on arms and chest, and swim off.
Although the current's against us, we're making
good headway. What a luxury to stretch our arms,
to snort, gurgle, splash, and to flail out around us.
Past Wesseling the water is clear.
Seagulls escort us a while.
When we turn on our backs, we talk about
what will await us. I pinch Angela's arm.
We're not dreaming. At the Lorelei cliff we actually do
meet a fisherman in his rowboat.
He's taking his time so that he can converse.
Later he invites us into his boat.
Mary especially arouses his interest.
She looks exactly like a certain someone.
Sometimes he looks her in the face. Until past Bingen
he rows us. He hesitates to come with us.
On the one hand, he sees our historical chance;
on the other, he has a wife and children.
While we are waving to him, the boat and cap become
smaller and smaller. Toward evening we reach Mainz.

Von weitem schon sehen wir die Fahnen am Ufer.
Die Rote Hilfe begrüßt uns, reicht Decken
Frottiertücher. Wie mir die Knie zittern.

ALLE LEICHTIGKEIT FORT

Alle Leichtigkeit fort
Schnee pappt grau an den Sohlen
Du liebtest eine Zwergin
Die wuchs.

MATHEMATIK DER FRAUENBEWEGUNG:
ZWEIMAL FRAU GLEICH FRAU?

wenn eine frau,
die zum manne X im verhältnis arbeiterin—chef steht,
soviel wut in ihrem bauch angesammelt hat,
daß sie ihn in die luft sprengt,
und wenn dann frau,
die zu dem selben mann X
    im verhältnis ehefrau-ehetyrann steht,
nach dem tode ihres mannes die firma übernimmt,
in welchem verhältnis steht dann frau zu frau?

From afar we see the flags on the shoreline.
The Red Relief Squad greets us, gives us blankets,
terrycloth towels. How my knees shake!

—S.L. Cocalis

ALL OF THE EASINESS GONE

All of the easiness gone
Snow pastes gray the soles
You loved a dwarf.
She grew.

—S.L. Cocalis

SIGRID WEIGEL (1950–)

MATHEMATICS FOR THE WOMEN'S MOVEMENT: DOES TWO TIMES WOMAN EQUAL WOMAN?

if a woman,
whose relationship to man X is that of worker : boss,
has collected so much anger inside her
that she blows him to pieces,
and if then a woman,
whose relationship to the same man X
  was that of wife: tyrannical husband,
takes over the company after his death,
what will be the relationship of woman to woman?

—S.L. Cocalis

NAMEN

Luzifer
hast du dich genannt
weil du listig und stark sein wolltest

Lucia
hast du dich genannt
weil du strahlen und leuchten wolltest

Lucy
steht jetzt auf deinem Grabstein

Kindchen
hat mein Vater dich immer genannt

Ich
habe dich Mama genannt

AN MEINE MÜTTER

Diesmal werde ich
mich selbst gebären
Endlich werde ich meine
Mutter
ausstoßen
wie eine lang zurückgehaltene
Nachgeburt
Ich werde mich
erlösen von der
Tyrannei
ihres verwundenden Blutes
in dem ich schwimme
seit ich die Nacht
ihrer Welt erblickt

MARIA NEEF-UTHOFF (1947–)

NAMES

Lucifer
you called yourself
because you wanted to be cunning and strong

Lucia
you called yourself
because you wanted to radiate light

Lucy
is written on your tombstone

My child
my father always called you

I
called you Mama

—*S.L. Cocalis*

SIGRID AMMER (n.d.)

TO MY MOTHERS

This time I will
bear myself
Finally I will
expel
my mother
like a long held-in
placenta
I will free
myself from the
tyranny
of her wounded blood
in which I swim
since I saw the night
of her world

In der Mitte meines Lebens
geht mir
der Stern auf
Laß uns dem Stern folgen
da wird auch
ein Tag werden endlich
Land in mein Auge fallen
und ein Gehöft sich finden
Dort werde ich mir selbst
das Leben geben
Mit deiner Hilfe
Mutter
bringe ich mich
zu meiner Welt

In the middle of my life
my star
is rising
Let us follow the star
there a new day
will finally dawn
Land will hit my eye
and I'll find a farm
There I will give birth
to myself
With your help
mother
I will bring myself
into my world

—S.L. Cocalis

NOTES ON THE POETS

Sigrid Ammer (n.d.)
Sigrid Ammer is a contemporary poet. "An meine Mütter" appeared in
Frauenoffensive 11 (July 1978).

Louise Aston (1814–1871)
Influenced by the democratic ideals of the revolutionary movement as well
as by George Sand's ideas on sexual emancipation, Louise Aston was
notorious for her own free lifestyle and the radical views she espoused
in her novels, essays, and poetry. In 1846 she was banned from Berlin on
moral grounds. After the March Revolution of 1848, Aston returned to edit
the revolutionary paper *Der Freischärler*, but it was eventually suppressed
and she was banned from Berlin a second time. After 1850 she resigned
herself to the political status quo and stopped publishing almost entirely.
Her principal works include *Wilde Rosen: Zwölf Gedichte* (1846); pieces in
Der Freischärler: Für Kunst und sociales Leben, which she edited in 1848; and
Freischärler-Reminiscenzen: Zwölf Gedichte (1850).

Ingeborg Bachmann (1926–1973)
Ingeborg Bachmann was an Austrian poet known also for her radio plays
and short stories. She studied philosophy, working with the "Viennese
School" associated with Ludwig Wittgenstein, and wrote her doctoral the-
sis on Martin Heidegger. She began publishing poetry in 1953, and soon
became one of the most prominent poets writing in German. She traveled
extensively and lived in France, Germany, Switzerland, and Italy, where
she died in a fire. Her principal works include the poems collected in *Die
gestundete Zeit* (1953) and *Anrufung des großen Bären* (1956); short stories
collected in *Das dreißigste Jahr* (1961), translated into English as *The Thir-
tieth Year* (1964), and *Simultan* (1972); two radio plays, *Der gute Gott von
Manhattan—Die Zikaden* (1963); a novel *Malina* (1971); "Frankfurter
Vorlesungen," on the problems of contemporary writing (published 1980);
and the unfinished *Der Fall Franza—Requiem für Fanny Goldmann* (1979). Her
work is collected in *Werke*, 4 vols, edited by C. Koschel, I.V. Weidenbaum,
and C. Münster (1982).

Margarete Beutler (1876–1949)
A teacher, translator, and editor of the magazine *Jugend*, Margarete Beutler
published poetry, plays, and short prose works in the first decades of this
century. Her works include *Gedichte* (1903), *Neue Gedichte* (1908), and *Leb'
wohl, Boheme!* (1911).

Emma Döltz (1866–1950)

Emma Döltz spent most of her life in a working-class milieu in Berlin and became politically active as a Socialist and feminist in the 1890s. After 1894, her poetry and short stories appeared regularly in the feminist periodical *Gleichheit*, edited by Clara Zetkin. Döltz's principal collection of poems is titled *Jugend-Lieder* (1900).

Annette von Droste-Hülshoff (1797–1848)

Renowned as "Germany's greatest woman poet" during her lifetime, Annette von Droste-Hülshoff was untouched by the political upheavals of her day. She grew up in the conservative Catholic atmosphere of the Westphalian landed gentry, was educated by private tutors, and began to write at an early age, though opposed in this by her father. After his death, friends encouraged her to publish. Her second volume of poetry, published in 1844, drew critical acclaim and established her as a major poet of her day. All of her work is collected in *Sämtliche Werke*, edited by C. Heselhaus (4th ed., 1963).

Marie von Ebner-Eschenbach (1830–1916)

Marie von Ebner-Eschenbach, Countess Dubsky, grew up spending summers on the family estate in Moravia and winters in Vienna. Impressed by the productions of the Viennese Burgtheater, she decided to become a dramatist. Though this wish was never realized, she did become a prolific and recognized author of prose fiction and essays. She also published poetry and a collection of aphorisms. Her work is collected in *Gesammelte Schriften* (1893).

Ute Erb (1940–)

Ute Erb lived in the German Democratic Republic (GDR) until 1957, and is primarily known for her poetry depicting problems of the working class, for her contributions to the *Sendung Freies Berlin*, and for her translations. She has worked as a typesetter and proofreader and been active in her union, in the organization of West German writers, and in various political causes. Her works include *Die Kette am Hals: Aufzeichnungen eines zornigen jungen Mädchens aus Mitteldeutschland* (1960) and *Ein schöner Land: Gedichte* (1976).

Barbara Fiedler (1942–)

A writer and teacher living in Bremen, Barbara Fiedler contributes regularly to the women's literary journals *Eva* and *schreiben* and has been active in organizing conferences for West German women writers. "Abstammung" appeared in *Frauenoffensive* 11 (July 1978).

Frederike Frei (1945–)

A poet living in Hamburg, Frederike Frei has been experimenting with alternative methods of mediating poetry. She has peddled individual poems in postcard format at the Frankfurt Book Fair, women's gatherings, and the Dokumenta Exhibitions in Kassel. Her most recent endeavor is a *Literaturpostamt* (*Literary Post Office*), which mails out poems to subscribers on requested topics. "Streicheleinheiten" appeared in *Frauenoffensive* 11 (July 1978). She has also published two collections of poetry, *Losgelebt* and *Betr. Liebe* (1986).

Catharina Regina von Greiffenberg (1633–1694)
One of the most prestigious women poets of the German Baroque era, Catharina Regina von Greiffenberg was educated in the Renaissance tradition by her uncle, who also saw to the publication of her works and later married her. She was known for her religious sonnets, sacred songs, and poems but also wrote a nationalistic epic, set in the times of the Turkish Wars. After her husband's death, Greiffenberg was forced into exile for religious reasons and took up residence in Nuremberg. There she was invited to join various literary societies, such as Siegmund von Birken's Pegnesischer Blumenorden. She was the first female member of Philipp von Zesen's Deutschgesinnter Genossenschaft. Her works are collected in *Sieges-Seule der Buße und des Glaubens* (1675) and *Geistliche Sonette, Lieder und Gedichte* (1662, reprinted 1967).

Argula von Grumbach (1492–1554)
Argula von Grumbach, née Staufer, published "Ain Antwort in Gedichth..." in Rome in 1523.

Karoline von Günderode (1780–1806)
Karoline von Günderode entered a *Damenstift*, an institution for Protestant women of rank, in Frankfurt and lived there until her death. There she pursued studies in mythology, philosophy, and anthropology and wrote her poetry, plays, and prose pieces. Through her writing, she tries to attain a romantic synthesis of philosophy, mythology, and art. Suffering from an unhappy love for a married man, she died by her own hand. Her work is collected in *Gesammelte Dichtungen*, edited by E. Salomon (1923); *Gesammelte Werke*, 3 vols. (1920–22, reprinted 1970); and *Der Schatten eines Traumes: Gedichte, Prosa, Briefe, Zeugnisse von Zeitgenossen*, edited by Christa Wolf (1981).

Ida Hahn-Hahn (1805–1880)
While her father sacrificed the family's considerable fortune to his passion for the theater, Ida Hahn-Hahn married a rich cousin in 1826, divorced him in 1829, and never remarried. Thereafter she traveled extensively, sometimes with a male companion, and became a prolific author of travelogues, novels, poetry, short stories, and memoirs. She is primarily known for her novels, which were exceedingly popular in her day. Her heroines are often exponents of emancipated views, especially in respect

to love, marriage, divorce, and rearing children. In 1850 Hahn-Hahn converted to Catholicism and eventually founded a convent in which she herself lived as a lay sister. Her poetry is available in *Musenalmanach für das Jahr 1831* and in her volume *Neue Gedichte* (1836); the novels of her Protestant period in the *Gesamtausgabe*, 21 vols. (1851) and those of her Catholic period in *Gesammelte Werke*, 45 vols, edited by O. von Schaching (1902–1905).

Anna Owena Hoyers (1584–1655)
Daughter of a famous astronomer, Anna Owena Hoyers enjoyed an unusual education for a woman of her time, including studies in Latin, Greek, and Hebrew. After the death of her husband in 1622, she began to espouse Anabaptist religious causes in pamphlets, letters, didactic and satiric pieces, and hymns. Hoyers gained a certain amount of recognition for her writings and was supported by the Swedish court. A selection of her works published in 1650 was burned in many places for its heretical views. Her best work appears in *Geistliche und weltliche Poemata* (1650.)

Marie Janitschek (1859–1927)
Of Hungarian origin, Marie Janitschek began publishing as a journalist in Graz under the pseudonym Marius Stern. After her marriage in 1892 she turned to more literary endeavors, treating the relationship between the sexes and especially themes taken from the Old Testament in her naturalistic poems, stories, novellas, and novels. Her poems are found in *Irdische und unirdische Träume* (1889), *Gesammelte Gedichte* (1892), and *Gedichte* (1917). Her stories are collected in *Legenden und Geschichten* (1885), *Lichthungrige Leute* (1892), and *Pfadsucher* (1894). She also wrote the novels *Ins Leben verirrt* (1898), *Die neue Eva* (1902), *Mimikry* (1903), and *Im Finstern* (1910).

Mascha Kaléko (1912–1975)
Studying and working in Berlin, Mascha Kaléko was "discovered" in 1930 and thereafter contributed poems regularly to the Berlin papers. She soon became famous throughout Germany for her ironic depiction of urban life and her satiric wit, tempered by an essentially romantic and melodic style. In 1938 she was forced to emigrate, and lived in New York and Jerusalem until her death. Her works include *Das lyrische Stenogrammheft* (1933), *Kleines Lesebuch für Große* (1934), both reprinted in 1956, and *Verse für Zeitgenossen* (1945, reprinted 1980).

Anna Louisa Karsch (1722–1791)
The first German woman to support herself by her pen, Anna Louisa Karsch came from a poor peasant background in Silesia and was taught to read and write by her great-uncle. This education was soon interrupted as she had to work on the farm. Her first marriage ended in divorce; her

second husband was an alcoholic. Karsch began writing occasional verse to support herself and her seven children; she became known at the court of Frederick the Great and was eventually brought to Berlin and introduced into the literary circles of the day. The enormous popularity of her poetry enabled her to live from her writing. Her work is collected in *Auserlesene Gedichte* (1764, reprinted 1966).

Marie Luise Kaschnitz (1901–1974)
Marie Luise Kaschnitz grew up in Potsdam and Berlin in an aristocratic family, worked in bookstores, and married an archaeologist. During the war she began writing prose fiction and essays, and then poetry during the post-war years. Her books of poetry include *Gedichte* (1947), *Totentanz und Gedichte zur Zeit* (1947), *Zukunftsmusik* (1950), *Ewige Stadt* (1952), *Neue Gedichte* (1957), *Dein Schweigen—Meine Stimme: Gedichte 1958–61* (1962), and *Kein Zauberspruch* (1972). She has also written the novels *Liebe beginnt* (1933) and *Elissa* (1937), and short stories collected in *Das dicke Kind* (1952) and *Lange Schatten* (1960). Her memoirs appear in the volumes *Engelsbrücke* (1955) and *Das Haus der Kindheit* (1956).

Karin Kiwus (1942–)
Karin Kiwus studied journalism, German, and political science; worked for Radio Bremen, Sender Freies Berlin, and as an editorial assistant for a publishing house; and is currently heading the Literature Department of the Academy of the Arts, West Berlin. She has won general critical recognition for her poetry, collected in *Von beiden Seiten der Gegenwart* (1976) and *Angenommen Später* (1979).

Gertrud Kolmar (1894–1943?)
Member of a prominent Jewish family in Berlin, Gertrud Kolmar (actual name: Chodziesner) led a reclusive existence, writing poetry from an early age. Fluent in French and English, she served as an interpreter at a prisoner-of-war camp during World War I; she later taught disabled children. Kolmar wrote a long sequence of poems in 1927 and 1928, published in 1934 as *Preußische Wappen*. From 1927 to 1937 she worked on three cycles of poems: *Weibliches Bildnis*, *Kind*, and *Tierträume*, published in 1938 as *Die Frau und die Tiere*. The two poems included here are among the seventy-five of the *Weibliches Bildnis* cycle portraying woman in her various ages, roles, and symbolic transformations. Hounded out of her family home and doing forced labor in a Berlin factory, she wrote her last poems in Hebrew before being deported to a concentration camp and disappearing in 1943. Her work is collected in *Das lyrische Werk*, edited by F. Kemp (1960).

Ursula Krechel (1947–)
After studying the theater and German at the university, Ursula Krechel

joined the West German women's movement in 1973 and has published many poems and essays on this topic. Today she lives as an independent writer in Darmstadt. Known primarily for her poetry and essays, she has also written a play, *Erika* (1974), and radio and television scripts. Among her works are *Selbsterfahrung und Fremdbestimmung: Bericht aus der Neuen Frauenbewegung* (1976), *Nach Mainz!* (1977), and *Verwundbar wie in den besten Zeiten* (1979).

Margaretha Susanna von Kuntsch (1651–1716)
Educated by her father, a court official, in Latin, French, and other subjects, Margaretha Susanna von Kuntsch married a counselor to the court and had fourteen children. Her poetry deals mostly with the deaths of thirteen of those children. The rest of the poems describe life at court. Her work is collected in *Sämtliche Geist- und weltliche Gedichte* (1720).

Berta Lask (1878–1967)
A Communist and pacifist primarily known for her political dramas and prose work, Berta Lask also wrote lyric poetry influenced by German expressionism and the women's movement. She continued to write agitatory poems for proletarian periodicals until her arrest in 1933. Upon her release, she emigrated to the Soviet Union and eventually settled in East Berlin. Among her poetry collections are *Stimmen* (1919) and *Rufe aus dem Dunkel: Auswahl 1915–1921* (1921). She is also known for her dramas *Die Päpstin* (1906), *Auf dem Hof, vier Treppen links* (1912), *Thomas Münzer* (1925), and *Leuna 1921* (1926), and her novel *Stille und Sturm* (1955).

Mechthild von Magdeburg (1210–1285)
Mechthild von Magdeburg was one of the most famous German mystics of the thirteenth century. She lived as a Beguine in Magdeburg from 1230 to 1270, wrote her prose and poetry there, and was instrumental in the instruction of other young women. Her writing is characterized by the theme of divine *Minne*, or courtly love addressed to God. Her work is collected in *Fließendes Licht der Gottheit*, 6 vols. (1250–64).

Angelika Mechtel (1943–)
One of the most prominent contemporary woman writers in the Federal Republic of Germany (FRG), Angelika Mechtel has always been an outspoken feminist and critic of society in general. Although she is primarily known and critically acclaimed for her short stories and novels, she has also written poetry, essays, and scripts for radio and television. Her poems have been published in *Gegen Eis und Flut* (1963), *Lachschärpe* (1965), and *Meine zärtlichste Freundin* (1981). Her novels include *Kaputte Spiele* (1971), *Friß Vogel* (1972), *Die Blindgängerin* (1974), *Wir sind arm, Wir sind reich* (1977), *Die andere Hälfte der Welt oder Frühstücksgespräche mit Paula* (1980), and *Gott und die Liedermacherin* (1983). She has also collected her

short stories in the volumes *Die feinen Totengräber* (1968), *Hochhausgeschichten* (1971), *Die Träume der Füchsin* (1976), and *Keep Smiling* (1977).

Klara Müller-Jahnke (1860–1905)
Klara Müller-Jahnke began writing as a form of political protest against the oppressive conditions of her workplace. Her often emotionally phrased Socialist poetry was published by the proletarian presses. Her works include *Mit roten Kressen* (1899), *Sturmlieder vom Meer* (1901), *Gesammelte Gedichte*, 2 vols. (1907), and *Wach auf! Letzte Gedichte* (1907).

Marie von Najmájer (1844–1904)
A Viennese writer of Hungarian descent, Marie von Najmájer was encouraged to write by Franz Grillparzer. Although she did not formally associate herself with the women's movement, her poetry, tales, and plays often portray independent, intellectual women. Later in life she provided financial assistance to women wishing to pursue higher education or a career in the arts. Her works include *Schneeglöckchen* (1868), *Gedichte* (1872), and *Neue Gedichte* (1891).

Maria Neef-Uthoff (1947–)
Maria Neef-Uthoff is a poet and journalist living in West Berlin. She has been active in the West German women's movement and has contributed regularly to feminist journals. She is currently working as an editor for *Tageszeitung (taz)*. "Namen" appeared in *Frauenoffensive* 11 (July 1978).

Helga M. Novak (1935–)
Helga M. Novak studied philosophy and journalism in Leipzig and has · lived in the GDR, Iceland, and the FRG. Widely acclaimed for her short stories and poetry, Novak received the literary prize of the city of Bremen in 1968. Her poetry collections include *Ballade von der reisenden Anna* (1965), *Colloquium mit vier Häuten* (1967), *Balladen vom kurzen Prozeß* (1975), and *Margarete mit dem Schrank* (1978). She has also published collections of short stories, *Geselliges Beisammensein* (1968), *Aufenthalt in einem irren Haus* (1971), and *Die Landnahme von Torre Bela* (1976).

Helga Osswald (1942–)
Helga Osswald left the GDR in 1959 and now teaches in Heidelberg. "Ein Zeuge" appeared in *Bewegte Frauen*, edited by R. Mayer (1977).

Louise Otto-Peters (1819–1895)
One of the most outspoken advocates of women's emancipation in the nineteenth century, Louise Otto-Peters began writing on social themes in 1840 under the pseudonym Otto Stern. In 1847 she delineated a plan for a German women's movement, began organizing groups to this effect,

and founded the first *Deutsche Frauenzeitung* two years later. In 1865 she helped initiate the Allgemeiner deutscher Frauenverein, which became the underlying organization of the bourgeois women's movement. Her works of poetry include *Lieder eines deutschen Mädchens* (1847), *Gedichte* (1868), and *Mein Lebensgang: Gedichte aus fünf Jahrzehnten* (1893). She also published many socially critical novels, including *Ludwig der Kellner* (1843) and *Schloß und Fabrik* (1847). Her most significant works on the history of the women's movement are *Das Recht der Frauen auf Erwerb* (1866), *Frauenleben im Deutschen Reich* (1876), and *Das erste Vierteljahrhundert des Allgemeinen Deutschen Frauenvereins* (1890).

Betty Paoli (1814–1894)

Betty Paoli, whose actual name was Elisabeth Glück, worked as a governess, tutor, and social companion in aristocratic families in Vienna and also had time to pursue her poetic endeavors. Many of her poems deal with unhappy love and were received as an expression of "true womanhood"; others were criticized for their unusual daring. She was also acclaimed for her essays and her translations of Ivan Turgenev. Her best poems are found in *Gedichte* (1841), *Nach dem Gewitter* (1843), and *Gedichte: Auswahl und Nachlaß*, edited by Marie von Ebner-Eschenbach (1895).

Ida von Reinsberg-Düringsfeld (1815–1876)

Primarily known for her prose fiction and essays on linguistic and cultural topics, Ida von Reinsberg-Düringsfeld also published lyric poetry under the pseudonym Thekla; her collection is entitled *Für Dich: Lieder* (1851).

Margot Schroeder (1937–)

Margot Schroeder gave up her job in a bookstore to become a housewife and take care of her two children. After a while she began writing for the radio and then won international recognition for her first novel, *Ich stehe meine Frau* (1975). Schroeder views herself as a member of the working class and as a committed feminist, and her works reflect her convictions. Her poetry is collected in *Die Angst ist baden gegangen* (1976). She has also written a second novel, *Der Schlachter empfiehlt noch immer Herz* (1976).

Verena Stefan (1947–)

Born in Switzerland, Verena Stefan has lived in West Berlin since 1968, where she studied physical therapy and sociology. *Häutungen*, her collection of "autobiographical sketches, poems, dreams, analyses" (1975) caused an immediate sensation in the German literary world and was heralded as a major breakthrough in women's writing. She has also written a volume of poetry titled *Mit Füßen und Flügeln* (1980) and has published essays on writing in *Frauenoffensive* and *Die Zeit*.

Anna Helena Volckmann (c. 1736)

All we know of Anna Helena Volckmann is her book, *Erstlinge Unvollkommener Gedichte*, published in Leipzig in 1736, which contains her letter to Christiana Mariana von Ziegler.

J. Monika Walther (1945–)

J. Monika Walther studied journalism, history, pedagogy, and psychology, and started a small feminist press, the Verlag Frauenpolitik. Later she founded the Tende Press. She has published *Ein Paar Dinge von denen ich weiß* (1977) and *Verlorene Träume: Geschichten nach dem Hochzeitslied* (1978).

H. E. Weichmann (eighteenth century)

Wife of the publicist C. F. Weichmann, H. E. Weichmann wrote in the first half of the eighteenth century. ''Über Mademoiselle Weichmann ungemeine Geschicklichkeit...'' first appeared in *C. F. Weichmanns Poesie der Nieder-Sachsen, oder allerhand mehrenteils noch nie gedruckte Gedichte von den behrühmtesten Nieder-Sachsen, sonderlich einigen ansehnlichen Mit-Gliedern der vormals in Hamburg blühenden Teutschübenden Gesellschaft*, vol. 4 (1732).

Sigrid Weigel (1950–)

Sigrid Weigel studied German and sociology and now is a professor of German and women's studies at the University of Hamburg. In collaboration with colleagues, Weigel has been instrumental in implementing courses in women's studies in German universities. She and other Germanists founded the group Frauen in der Literaturwissenschaft in 1983. She has published numerous essays on feminist interpretations of German women writers.

Gabriele Wohmann (1932–)

Gabriele Wohmann studied German and taught at a boarding school before devoting herself entirely to writing. Over the years she has gained an international following for her satirically realistic, ironic indictment of the middle class. Wohmann's novels, which seem to be more autobiographical than her short stories, can often be found on the bestseller lists in the FRG. She also writes for radio and television. Wohmann has received numerous prizes and grants, and continues to write prolifically. Her poems are collected in *So ist die Lage* (1974), and her short stories in *Sämtliche Erzählungen* (1980). Her novels include *Jetzt und nie* (1958), *Abschied für länger* (1969), *Ernste Absicht* (1970), *Paulinchen war allein zu Haus* (1974), *Schönes Gehege* (1975), *Ausflug mit der Mutter* (1976), *Frühherbst in Badenweiler* (1978), and *Ach wie gut, daß niemand weiß* (1980).

Sidonie Hedwig Zäunemann (1714–1740)

One of the first female poets to be influenced by Christiana Mariana von

Ziegler, Sidonie Hedwig Zäunemann was, like her, crowned poet laureate by the University of Göttingen. In her works she defends her independent lifestyle and poetic ambitions. Donning men's clothing, she would ride about the countryside on horseback and then compose poems about what she had observed. Zäunemann's poems are collected in two volumes: *Poetische Rosen in Knospen* (1732) and *Die von denen Faunen gepeitschte Laster* (1739).

Susanna Elisabeth Zeidler (c. 1686)
Daughter of a pastor in the small town of Fienstedt, Susanna Elisabeth Zeidler published her only volume of poetry in 1686, *Jungferlicher Zeitvertreiber*, occasional and devotional poems. As her father stresses in the dedication, writing these poems did not detract from the performance of her domestic duties.

Christiana Mariana von Ziegler (1695–1760)
Christiana Mariana von Ziegler entered the cultural life of Leipzig with her musical salon in 1722, but soon began to write poetry, essays, dialogues, and fables. J. S. Bach set some of her early poems to music, and J. G. Gottsched sponsored her as the first female member of the Deutsche Gesellschaft. Ziegler was also the first woman to be crowned poet laureate of a German university. Her published works are *Versuch in gebundener Schreib-Art* (1728) and *Vermischete Schriften in gebundener und ungebundener Rede* (1739).

Kathinka Zitz-Halein (1801–1877)
Educated in boarding schools, Kathinka Halein eventually found work as a governess and tutor. Later she married Franz Zitz, a member of the Frankfurt Parliament and a leader of the revolutionary movement in Mainz. In her poetry, which she produced continually in an effort to support the family, she criticized the political, social, and ecclesiastical conditions of her day. She also published numerous novels and stories. Her poetry is collected in *Herbstrosen in Poesie und Prosa* (1846) and *Dur- und Molltöne* (1859).

ACKNOWLEDGMENTS

We gratefully acknowledge permission to include the German texts and English translations of the following poems:

SIGRID AMMER: "An meine Mütter." Reprinted from *Frauenoffensive* 11 (July 1978) by permission of the editors of *Frauenoffensive Journal*.

INGEBORG BACHMANN: "Wahrlich" and "Alle Tage" from her *Werke*. Munich: Piper Verlag, 1978. By permission of the publisher.

ANNETTE VON DROSTE-HÜLSHOFF: "On the Tower" translated by Ruth Angress. By permission of the translator.

UTE ERB: "Sozialismus, sag ich" and "Ein Ungenügen" from her volume *Ein schöner Land*. Berlin: Fietkau Verlag, 1976. By permission of the publisher.

BARBARA FIEDLER: "Abstammung." Reprinted from *Frauenoffensive* 11 (July 1978). By permission of the poet.

FREDERIKE FREI: "Streicheleinheiten." Reprinted from *Frauenoffensive* 11 (July 1978). By permission of the poet.

MARIE LUISE KASCHNITZ: "Die Katze" from her volume *Neue Gedichte* (1957). "Nur die Augen" from her volume *Dein Schweigen—Meine Stimme* (1962). "Frauenfunk" from her volume *Kein Zauberspruch* (1972). By permission of the Claasen Verlag in Düsseldorf.

KARIN KIWUS: "Aufklärungsstunde," "Hommes à femme," and "Make-off" from her volume *Von beiden Seiten der Gegenwart*. Frankfurt a/M: Suhrkamp, 1976. By permission of the publisher.

GERTRUD KOLMAR: "Die Dichterin" and "Die Unerschlossene" translated by Henry A. Smith from *Dark Soliloquy: Selected Poems of Gertrud Kolmar*. New York: Continuum Publishing Company, 1975. By permission of the publisher.

URSULA KRECHEL: "Hymne auf die Frauen der bürgerlichen Klasse," "Warnung," and "Nach Mainz!" from her volume *Nach Mainz!* Neuwied/Darmstadt: Luchterhand Verlag, 1977. "Alle Leichtigkeit fort" from her volume *Verwundbar wie in den besten Zeiten*. Neuwied/Darmstadt: Luchterhand, 1979. By permission of the publisher.

ANGELIKA MECHTEL: "Den Reis kochen" from her volume *Meine zärtlichste Freundin*. Munich, 1981. "Die Kinder die sie" is reprinted from *Bewegte Frauen*, ed. R. Mayer. Zurich, 1977. Both poems reprinted by permission of the poet.

MARIA NEEF-UTHOFF: "Namen." Reprinted from *Frauenoffensive* 11 (July 1978). By permission of the *Frauenoffensive Journal*.

HELGA NOVAK: "Lagebericht," "Brief an Medea," and "Frühling im Westend" from her volume *Margarete mit dem Schrank*. Berlin: Rotbuch Verlag, 1978. By permission of the poet.

HELGA OSSWALD: "Ein Zeuge." Reprinted from *Bewegte Frauen*, ed. R. Mayer. Zurich, 1977. By permission of the poet.

MARGOT SCHROEDER: "Mir geht es gut" and "Ich denke an dich" from her volume *Die Angst ist baden gegangen*. Berlin: Fietkau Verlag, 1976. By permission of the publisher.

VERENA STEFAN: "Die frau, die sich im koitus mit bewegt" from *Häutungen*. Munich: Frauenoffensive Verlag, 1975. By permission of the author. Translated by Johanna Moore and Beth Weckmueller in *Shedding*. New York: Daughters, Inc., 1978. By permission of the translators.

J. MONIKA WALTHER: "meine vorletzte rede..." reprinted from *Texte zum Anfassen: Frauenlesebuch*, ed. K. Reschke. Munich, 1978. By permission of the poet.

SIGRID WEIGEL: "mathematik der frauenbewegung..." reprinted from *Texte zum Anfassen: Frauenlesebuch*, ed. K. Reschke. Munich, 1978. By permission of the poet.

GABRIELE WOHMANN: "Ich bin kein Insekt," "Übeltäter," and "Wieder ist alles gut gegangen" by permission of the poet. "Evildoer" and "Again Everything Has Gone Quite Well" translated by Margaret Woodruff, *Dimension* 1, no. 2 (1968), pp. 222–25. By permission of the editor of *Dimension*.

Except for those mentioned above, all translations were made especially for this book, and are used by permission of the translators.

The Feminist Press at The City University of New York offers alternatives in education and in literature. Founded in 1970, this non-profit, tax-exempt educational and publishing organization works to eliminate sexual stereotypes in books and schools and to provide literature with a broad vision of human potential. The publishing program includes reprints of important works by women, feminist biographies of women, and nonsexist children's books. Curricular materials, bibliographies, directories, and a quarterly journal provide information and support for students and teachers of women's studies. In-service projects help to transform teaching methods and curricula. Through publications and projects, The Feminist Press contributes to the rediscovery of the history of women and the emergence of a more humane society.

FEMINIST CLASSICS FROM THE FEMINIST PRESS

Antoinette Brown Blackwell: A Biography, by Elizabeth Cazden. $19.95 cloth, $9.95 paper.
Between Mothers and Daughters: Stories Across a Generation. Edited by Susan Koppelman. $8.95 paper.
Brown Girl, Brownstones, a novel by Paule Marshall. Afterword by Mary Helen Washington. $8.95 paper.
Call Home the Heart, a novel of the thirties, by Fielding Burke. Introduction by Alice Kessler-Harris and Paul Lauter and afterwords by Sylvia J. Cook and Anna W. Shannon. $8.95 paper.
Cassandra, by Florence Nightingale. Introduction by Myra Stark. Epilogue by Cynthia Macdonald. $3.50 paper.
The Changelings, a novel by Jo Sinclair. Afterwords by Nellie McKay; and by Johnnetta B. Cole and Elizabeth H. Oakes; biographical note by Elisabeth Sandberg. $8.95 paper.
The Convert, a novel by Elizabeth Robins. Introduction by Jane Marcus. $6.95 paper.
Daughter of Earth, a novel by Agnes Smedley. Afterword by Paul Lauter. $7.95 paper.
A Day at a Time: The Diary Literature of American Women from 1764 to the Present, edited and with an introduction by Margo Culley. $29.95 cloth, $12.95 paper.
The Defiant Muse: French Feminist Poems from the Middle Ages to the Present, a bilingual anthology edited and with an introduction by Domna C. Stanton. $29.95 cloth, $11.95 paper.
The Defiant Muse: German Feminist Poems from the Middle Ages to the Present, a bilingual anthology edited and with an introduction by Susan L. Cocalis. $29.95 cloth, $11.95 paper.
The Defiant Muse: Hispanic Feminist Poems from the Middle Ages to the Present, a bilingual anthology edited and with an introduction by Angel Flores and Kate Flores. $29.95 cloth, $11.95 paper.
The Defiant Muse: Italian Feminist Poems from the Middle Ages to the Present, a bilingual anthology edited by Beverly Allen, Muriel Kittel, and Keala Jane Jewell, and with an introduction by Beverly Allen. $29.95 cloth, $11.95 paper.
The Female Spectator, edited by Mary R. Mahl and Helene Koon. $8.95 paper.
Guardian Angel and Other Stories, by Margery Latimer. Afterwords by Nancy Loughridge, Meridel Le Sueur, and Louis Kampf. $8.95 paper.
I Love Myself When I Am Laughing . . . And Then Again When I Am Looking Mean and Impressive, by Zora Neale Hurston. Edited by Alice Walker with an introduction by Mary Helen Washington. $9.95 paper.
Käthe Kollwitz: Woman and Artist, by Martha Kearns. $7.95 paper.
Life in the Iron Mills and Other Stories, by Rebecca Harding Davis. Biographical interpretation by Tillie Olsen. $7.95 paper.
The Living Is Easy, a novel by Dorothy West. Afterword by Adelaide M. Cromwell. $8.95 paper.
Mother to Daughter, Daughter to Mother: A Daybook and Reader, selected and shaped by Tillie Olsen. $9.95 paper.
The Other Woman: Stories of Two Women and a Man. Edited by Susan Koppelman. $8.95 paper.
Portraits of Chinese Women in Revolution, by Agnes Smedley. Edited with an introduction by Jan MacKinnon and Steve MacKinnon and an afterword by Florence Howe. $5.95 paper.
Reena and Other Stories, selected short stories by Paule Marshall. $8.95 paper.
Ripening: Selected Work, 1927–1980, by Meridel Le Sueur. Edited with an introduction by Elaine Hedges. $8.95 paper.

Rope of Gold, a novel of the thirties, by Josephine Herbst. Introduction by Alice Kessler-Harris and Paul Lauter and afterword by Elinor Langer. $8.95 paper.

The Silent Partner, a novel by Elizabeth Stuart Phelps. Afterword by Mari Jo Buhle and Florence Howe. $8.95.

Swastika Night, a novel by Katharine Burdekin. Introduction by Daphne Patai. $8.95 paper.

These Modern Women: Autobiographical Essays from the Twenties. Edited with an introduction by Elaine Showalter. $4.95 paper.

The Unpossessed, a novel of the thirties, by Tess Slesinger. Introduction by Alice Kessler-Harris and Paul Lauter and afterword by Janet Sharistanian. $8.95 paper.

Weeds, a novel by Edith Summers Kelley. Afterword by Charlotte Goodman. $7.95 paper.

A Woman of Genius, a novel by Mary Austin. Afterword by Nancy Porter. $8.95 paper.

The Woman and the Myth: Margaret Fuller's Life and Writings, by Bell Gale Chevigny. $8.95 paper.

Women and Appletrees, a novel by Moa Martinson. Translated from the Swedish and with an afterword by Margaret S. Lacy. $8.95 paper.

The Yellow Wallpaper, by Charlotte Perkins Gilman. Afterword by Elaine Hedges. $4.50 paper.

OTHER TITLES FROM THE FEMINIST PRESS

All The Women Are White, All The Blacks Are Men, But Some of Us Are Brave: Black Women's Studies. Edited by Gloria T. Hull, Patricia Bell Scott, and Barbara Smith. $12.95.

Black Foremothers: Three Lives, by Dorothy Sterling. $8.95 paper.

Complaints and Disorders: The Sexual Politics of Sickness, by Barbara Ehrenreich and Deirdre English. $3.95 paper.

The Cross-Cultural Study of Women. Edited by Margot I. Duley and Mary I. Edwards. $29.95 cloth, $12.95 paper.

Feminist Resources for Schools and Colleges: A Guide to Curricular Materials, 3rd edition. Compiled and edited by Anne Chapman. $12.95 paper.

Household and Kin: Families in Flux, by Amy Swerdlow et al. $8.95 paper.

How to Get Money for Research, by Mary Rubin and the Business and Professional Women's Foundation. Foreword by Mariam Chamberlain. $6.95 paper.

In Her Own Image: Women Working in the Arts. Edited with an introduction by Elaine Hedges and Ingrid Wendt. $9.95 paper.

Integrating Women's Studies into the Curriculum: A Guide and Bibliography, by Betty Schmitz. $9.95 paper.

Las Mujeres: Conversations from a Hispanic Community, by Nan Elsasser, Kyle MacKenzie, and Yvonne Tixier y Vigil. $8.95 paper.

Lesbian Studies: Present and Future. Edited by Margaret Cruikshank. $9.95 paper.

Moving the Mountain: Women Working for Social Change, by Ellen Cantarow with Susan Gushee O'Malley and Sharon Hartman Strom. $8.95 paper.

Out of the Bleachers: Writings on Women and Sport. Edited with an introduction by Stephanie L. Twin. $9.95 paper.

Reconstructing American Literature: Courses, Syllabi, Issues. Edited by Paul Lauter. $10.95 paper.

Salt of the Earth, screenplay by Michael Wilson with historical commentary by Deborah Silverton Rosenfelt. $5.95 paper.

Witches, Midwives, and Nurses: A History of Women Healers, by Barbara Ehrenreich and Deirdre English. $3.95 paper.

With These Hands: Women Working on the Land. Edited with an introduction by Joan M. Jensen. $9.95 paper.

Woman's "True" Profession: Voices from the History of Teaching. Edited with an introduction by Nancy Hoffman. $9.95 paper.

Women Have Always Worked: A Historical Overview, by Alice Kessler-Harris. $8.95 paper.

Women Working: An Anthology of Stories and Poems. Edited and with an introduction by Nancy Hoffman and Florence Howe. $8.95 paper.

For free catalog, write to The Feminist Press at The City University of New York, 311 East 94 Street, New York, N.Y. 10128. Send individual book orders to The Feminist Press, P.O. Box 1654, Hagerstown, MD 21741. Include $1.75 postage and handling for one book and 75¢ for each additional book. To order using MasterCard or Visa, call: (800) 638-3030.